CW00552172

The Training Space Ltd
22 Barnwell Court
Mawsley
NN14 1FG
United Kingdom
www.thetrainingspace.co.uk
www.janeconsidine.com

Ordering Information:
Quantity sales. Special discounts are available on quantity purchases by corporations, associations, schools and others. For details, contact the publisher at the address above. Orders by trade bookstores and wholesalers.

Please contact:

The Training Space Ltd
Tel: (+44) 01536 410078
Email: info@thetrainingspace.co.uk
Web: www.thetrainingspace.co.uk

Every effort has been made to obtain the necessary permissions with reference to copyright materials, both illustrative and quoted. We apologise for any omissions in this respect and will be pleased to make appropriate acknowledgements in any future editions.

Printed in the UK.

First edition.

ISBN 978-1-9075814-7-2

Designed by James Hunter, Lee Akers & Toby Stubbs
www.studiokaioti.com

> " The magic of spelling
> is taking speech that is
> invisible and turning it
> visible and transportable.
> Together, let's cast a spell
> for the next generation
> to be intrigued and
> enthusiastic about words. "

Jane Considine

Acknowledgements

Thank you to the countless schools I visited to look closer at their approaches to teaching spelling.

In particular, I really appreciated meeting the children who were excited about spelling and obsessed with words. The most amount of insight for me personally was provided in schools located in socio-economically challenged areas that were bucking the national trend with excellent spelling results. My findings here were the most instrumental towards the shaping of 'The Spelling Book' series.

A genuine open-hearted expression of gratitude to our spelling research group who helped us to develop and trial material. Special mentions to: Lisa Spandrzyk, Vicki Thurstance, Claire Holland, Jennifer James, Laura Lelapi, Mandy Forshaw, Jude Temple, Maria Barker, Kayley Wallace, Nana Brago and Tanya Peacock. This really wouldn't have happened without the magic touch of Bronwen Hughes and her 'stickler for detail' attitude and thorough approach to 'get things done'. Also, thank you to Ellie Ralls for the extra glitter sprinkled along the way to ensure this book sparkles with more words and examples. A big thank you to Kerry Kane for bravely taking on the task of finding the lost files... losing them... and finding them again! A special acknowledgement to James Hunter, Toby Stubbs and Lee Akers, for years and years of design expertise and who are able to add colour, consistency and beauty to all the mess I throw at them.

Thank you to Ben in Year 2 who still makes me giggle out loud about how he spells country. Finally, I want to thank my husband, Ian, for reading early drafts, design ideas and keeping the children out of my hair, so I could get these books written.
He is my rock.

An extra special thank you to the following teachers who contributed to The Spelling Book, we could not have done it without you:

Bryony Shaw	Jessi Matthews	Lauren Chambers
Emma Lloyd-Tunstall	Julia Simmonds	Lauren Connolly
Jane Toyer	Kerenza Jelbert	Stacey Louise Martin

#HeartBurst ♥

> " My spelling is wobbly, it's good spelling but it wobbles, and the letters get in the wrong places. "
>
> *Winnie-the-Pooh, A.A. Milne*

> " When our spelling is perfect, it's invisible. But when it's flawed, it prompts strong negative associations. "
>
> *Marilyn Vos Savant*

> " Is a bad speller one who casts a wicked spell? "
>
> *Lucky, Roger McGough*

> " Anyone who dares to treat spelling as an adventure will find the journey rewarding. "
>
> *Spell it Out, David Crystal*

> " The English Language is full of words that are just waiting to be misspelled and the world is full of sticklers, ready to pounce. "
>
> *Between You and Me, Confessions of a Comma Queen, Mary Norris*

> " I always was the spelling bee champion. I always loved words. I always wanted to know what they meant, why you used them, who first said them. I was always interested in that. "
>
> *Brenda Lee – 1960's singer*

> " The story of English spelling is the story of thousands of people – some well-known, most totally unknown - who left a permanent linguistic fingerprint on our orthography. "
>
> *David Crystal*

> " Issuing a weekly spelling test is not teaching spelling. I repeat, testing is not teaching. "
>
> *Alex Quigley*

The Spelling Book

Transforming the Teaching of Spelling

Jane Considine

The Training Space
Transforming teaching and learning

About the Author

Jane Considine has been an education consultant for over 20 years. She specialises in the teaching of writing, reading and spelling.

Her best selling books *'The Write Stuff - Transforming the Teaching of Writing'* and *'Hooked on Books - Transforming the Teaching of Reading'* have been instrumental in improving the teaching of writing and reading in thousands of schools all over the world. Her systems-based approaches offer a solution to the quandary of how to teach spelling using practical and simple strategies that are easy to follow and implement. *'The Spelling Book - Transforming the Teaching of Spelling'* provides a year's worth of support for busy teachers to enable pupils to get their 'spell on'!

Jane is a very popular presenter, and trains thousands of teachers every year, all across the world. Anybody who has witnessed Jane in action finds the experience hard to forget. Her effervescence and her in-depth subject knowledge has been described as "very practical, seriously inspiring and transformative".

A devoted user of Twitter originating from Birmingham in the UK, she now lives in Northamptonshire with her four children, three cats, two dogs and one long-suffering husband.

Jane Considine

Introduction

Spelling is certainly tricky. One of the most unenviable jobs is teaching children how to spell. The English language contains well over a million words and has been affected by some 1,300 years of history.

As the National Curriculum reminds us, "*Most people read words more accurately than they spell them. The younger pupils are, the truer this is.*" Many of us work with children from differing backgrounds: those learning to spell where English is their mother tongue; those learning to spell where English is an additional language. For many years, the teaching of spelling has been garbled, vague and confusing. We can see it lacks clarity when Year 6 spelling results are analysed on a national level and pupils perform particularly poorly, with only 13% of pupils being able to spell 'coarse' correctly. (2017 SATs Results)

Are you worrying about spelling standards in your school? Struggling to find time to teach it well? Lacking a systematic, whole school approach?

Inside this book, you will discover a clear and systematic view for teaching spelling that will provide children with life-long strategies. We need to teach spelling logically so they understand how "probability matching"* of sounds heard to grapheme representation will strengthen their spelling.

One of the hardest parts of our teaching jobs is to enable pupils to see the magic of words, the patterns that sparkle inside them and how word wizardry can help transform the quality of their writing to new enchanting heights that will keep a reader spellbound.

Spelling can confuse us, confound us and can weigh us down with rules and exceptions. We need to foster a future generation of curious, excited spellers who enjoy finding patterns in the baffling complexities of English spelling. Many adults label themselves as 'bad spellers' and we need to replace that perception with a new found reality of being 'practically perfect spellers.' Spelling needs to be raised in profile, targeted specifically in terms of time and activity and be made an energising and positive aspect of the school curriculum. The intention of this book is more than a quick fix with a magic wand but rather a fundamental overhaul of a spelling curriculum that is rigorous, vibrant and valued.

'The Spelling Book' provides a coherent system for teaching spelling consistently and supports pupils to define what it means to be an effective speller. The underlying structure of the approach is based on the three zones of spelling. The patterns of spelling are explored through the **GROUPINGS**, the pressure of spelling is eased through the **IMPROVINGs** and the remembering and recall of spelling through the **ACQUIRINGs**. Is spelling caught or taught? Most definitely taught and this year-view of support will show you how teachers teach, model and define as pupils practise, explore and investigate.

* Term coined by Diane McGuinness

The Three Zones
of Spelling

1 | Patterns →

2 | Pressure →

3 | Remembering →

Contents

The Three Zones of Spelling

The Patterns of Spelling

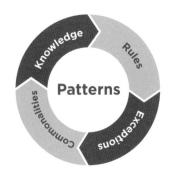

Patterns — Knowledge, Rules, Exceptions, Commonalities

Structures for Learning

THE GROUPINGS

The Pressure of Spelling

Pressure — Real Time, Edits, Independence, Logical

'In the Moment' Strategies

THE IMPROVINGs

The Remembering of Spelling

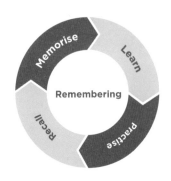

Remembering — Memorise, Learn, Practise, Recall

Strategies for Learning

THE ACQUIRINGs

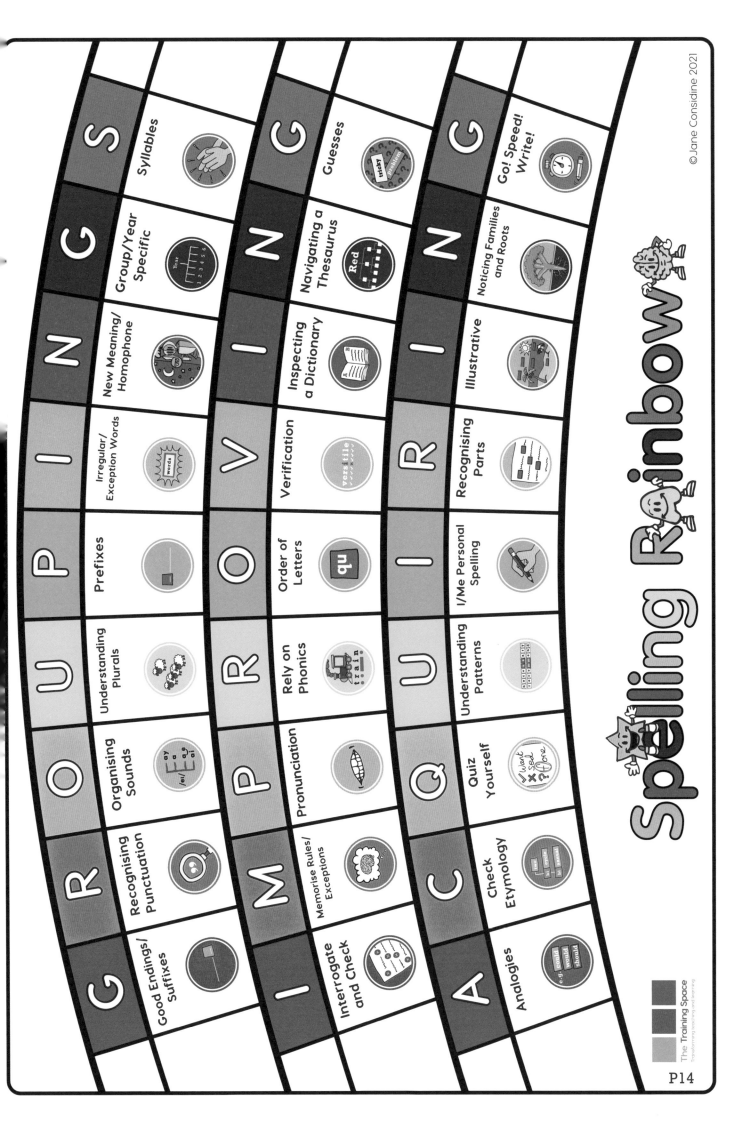

Spelling Rainbow

G – Good Endings/Suffixes
R – Recognising Punctuation
O – Organising Sounds
U – Understanding Plurals
P – Prefixes
I – Irregular/Exception Words
N – New Meaning/Homophone
G – Group/Year Specific
S – Syllables

I – Interrogate and Check
M – Memorise Rules/Exceptions
P – Pronunciation
R – Rely on Phonics
O – Order of Letters
V – Verification
I – Inspecting a Dictionary
N – Navigating a Thesaurus
G – Guesses

A – Analogies
C – Check Etymology
Q – Quiz Yourself
U – Understanding Patterns
I – I/Me Personal Spelling
R – Recognising Parts
I – Illustrative
N – Noticing Families and Roots
G – Go! Speed! Write!

© Jane Considine 2021

The Training Space
Transforming Teaching and Learning

P14

Super Stoked About Spelling

Schools that demand excellence in spelling prioritise it consistently and insist on high expectations for pupil performance. Spelling curriculums that work are grafted into the culture and climate of a school so much so that it 'zings' during teaching and learning exchanges about how to spell words. Words are great!

Top 10 Super-Stoked Strategies

1. Spelling T-Shirt

A few plain t-shirts are required with a sewn on clear polypocket. The spell of the day is worn by the teacher and promoted. The pupils' challenge is to put the spell of the day into their writing appropriately and spell it correctly. A new day... a new spell!

2. Spelling Scooters

A class prize to be won every term for the pupil who has made the most progress in spelling. The scooter is on display in every classroom and a beginning to end of term result is compared. The pupil that makes the most progress wins the scooter. This termly award can be altered to any prize within your budget.

3. Spelling Teams

Make mixed attainment groups of pupils within your class. Let the children name their teams, e.g. Word Wizards, Super Spellers, Dictionary Divas, Right Writers, etc. Take part in 10-20 word spelling tests but the aim of the game is to get a communal high score. Compete against other mixed attainment teams. The purpose of this is that all members have to help each other to excel and retain difficult spellings.

4. Spelling Hunts

At playtime, set up years 1-2, years 3-4 and years 5-6 'spelling hunts'. Pupils solve the clues but have to spell words accurately to unlock the prizes. The class with the highest results get extra playtime at the end of the term. For example, a teacher will write ten clues, hidden in envelopes around the play area, e.g. "A place where a horse lives?". The pupils then solve the clues with accurate spelling and place them in the 'Spell Prize Draw Post Box'.

5. Proud to Spell Properly

Celebration in assembly time that allows children to 'show off' in front of their friends that they can accurately spell really tricky words. They are awarded a 'Loud & Proud' spelling badge for their efforts.

6. Spelling Club

Pupils look at work by younger pupils and notice patterns and problems in their independent writing. They create a Top 10 of clangers or mistakes that pupils are making in their school in younger years. Older pupils run sessions of support and lead lessons to show others how to learn spellings and commit them to memory.

7. Silly Ditty/Dance

In assembly a child shows a silly way (maybe a bit cheeky or ridiculous) that helps them to remember a tricky word.

Do not embarrass yourself by forgetting the doubles!

8. Laminate Top 5 Spellings to Fix

This is written on using a whiteboard marker and is personalised to the child following editing or close analysis of the writing.

My Focus Five				
beautiful	because	disgusting	interesting	their

This is stuck on their desk and is a focus until corrected in their real independent writing. Words can be changed as they acquire them and show they can use them. Pupils squiggle/underline when they are using the word accurately in independent writing using a coloured gel pen.

9. Spelling Journals

These will help children build knowledge about words. They can record word lists, try out different strategies and record their thinking for future reference.

10. Spelling Mentors

Year 5 & 6 pupils, who are the best spellers, are kitted out with Collins English Dictionaries, electronic spelling machines or iPads and run lunchtime clubs to help pupils with their spelling problems. They chat with younger pupils about how they can learn tricky words and give them tips on how to improve.

WE ARE SPELLBOUND

Read with a 'switched on' brain 1

Be a phoneme finder and a syllable seeker 2

Seek patterns in sounds, letters and shapes 3

Say words slowly and clearly to hear the smallest of sounds 4

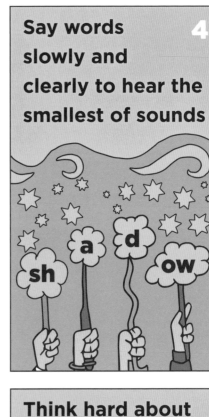

Think hard about logical and plausible options

6

Internalise letter sequences in words and know how from root words new words can be built 5

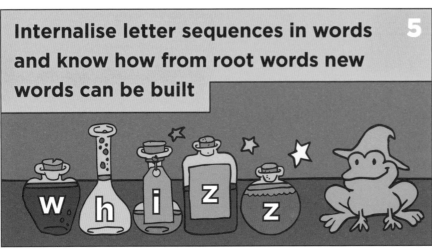

HOW TO USE THE
Spelling Book

To get the greatest benefit from this resource you will have to consider re-organising your timetable. Essentially, two different components of time need to be created across a fortnightly timetable.

During week one, a block of 50 minutes needs to be created to facilitate an investigation (30 minutes) and Go Grapheme Grafters (20 minutes). The nature of this is a 'slow' look at patterns and working to prove or disprove a hypothesis.

During week two, the same amount of time (50 minutes) is split into 5 x ten minute slots to experience pace and take a quicker look at spellings.

Please see the diagram overleaf that outlines the organisation and nature of this approach.

Guidance is provided for a year's worth of spelling material. Included are 18 investigations and 18 weeks of 10 minute, quick spelling experiences.

Pupils can collect medals of mastery once they have completed investigations, activities and fast tasks. You can find these at the back of the book. This approach will ensure your pupils will become **'Spelling Supremos'**.

Timetable

Week One

Investigation & Interleaving

1 x 30 minute slot/1 x 20 minute slot

Concocting and testing spells.

Deep - Slow - Pattern Finding

30 MINUTES

Using an investigative approach to understand the principles underpinning word construction (**phonemic**, **morphemic** and **etymological**) and test the hypothesis from the **GROUPINGS** layer of the **Spelling Rainbow**.

The purpose of this session is to facilitate pupils as word gatherers, word sorters, word pattern finders, word interrogators and word concluders.

Interleaving and Practice

20 MINUTES

The Go Grapheme Grafters tasks involve analysis of common errors, why these errors occur, and what to do to ensure that the correct spelling embeds in our long-term memory.

Organisation

Week Two

Daily Fast Task

5 x 10 minute slots

Exploring aspects from the **IMPROVINGs** and **ACQUIRINGs** layer of the Spelling Rainbow.

QUICK! | Monday
Short Burst Investigations
10 MINUTES

STICK! | Tuesday
Previous Year's Short Burst Investigations
10 MINUTES

FLICK! | Wednesday
Short Burst Investigations
10 MINUTES

TICK! | Thursday
Short Burst Investigations
10 MINUTES

CLICK! | Friday
Short Burst Investigations
10 MINUTES

20 MINUTES

GO GRAPHEME GRAFTERS!

Explained

The following pages are an overview of the thinking behind the 'Go Grapheme Grafters!' tasks which take twenty minutes per task and make up the interleaving and practice part of week one of your two week timetable. Test your pupils on these words. Keep a record of their scores.

Teach pupils these guiding principles to increase their bravery as spellers. Be aware as a teacher that rather than considering whether the spelling is right or wrong, move to a place where you analyse the tricky part of the word to spell. Using the 'Sound Association' information linked to every 'Go Grapheme Grafters!' page, share with your pupils that because they can spell 'what' they can spell 'was' as they know that the /ɒ/ phoneme can be written as the letter <a> in these words.

Phonics is your friend

- Every word is a collection of letters.
- These letters represent a speech sound.
- You must say the word SLOWLY and CLEARLY to hear the smallest units of sound. As you get older this can be 'in your head'.
- Practise segmenting words into its phonemes.

Phoneme	Grapheme
Smallest unit of sound in a word	Way of writing the phoneme using a letter or letters
1 phoneme = 1 grapheme 1 sound = 1 letter e.g. /æ/ in cat (1-1)	1 phoneme = digraph 1 sound = 2 letters e.g. /ʃ/ in shut (1-2)	1 phoneme = trigraph 1 sound = 3 letters e.g. /dʒ/ in judge (1-3)

- Listen carefully to the phonemes in words and assign the best choice of grapheme.
- Most sounds are represented by the most likely spelling of that sound and these are your 'best bets' when trying to spell a word.
- Some words have a mixture of phonemes that are easy to spell with one or two phonemes that are tricky.

Volatile vowels

- Consonant sounds are more stable (less options) and vowel sounds are more unstable (more options).
- Every vowel phoneme has at least two representations.

sit, crystal	wet, head	cat, plait	plot, swan	duck, some
put, could	banana, father	tree, knead	girl, learn	calf, hard
saw, taught	shoe, crew	play, eight	go, sew	sigh, my
loud, bough	boy, coin	fear, deer	there, their	pure, your

N.B. This list is not exhaustive.

- Some syllables are stressed and the vowel sounds are clear. In some words syllables are unstressed (vowel sounds less clear) and we hear it as /ə/. This sound is known as 'schwa' and can cause spelling difficulties, e.g. garden, teacher, amazing and cinema. This makes it difficult to identify which vowels to use, resulting in spelling mistakes.

Morphology

Notice common letter patterns and how words can be built around 11,000 root words and can change with different prefixes and suffixes, e.g.

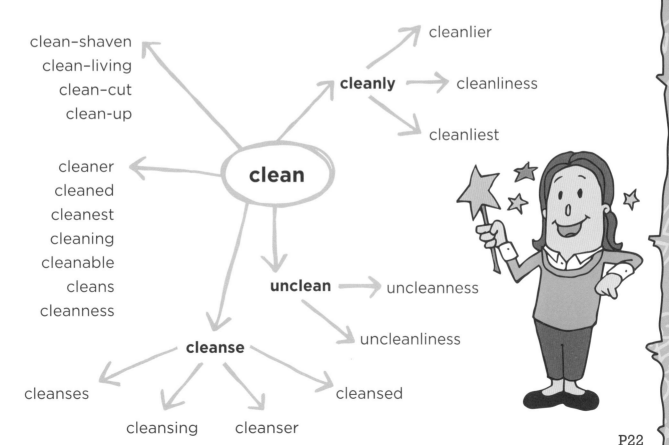

clean-shaven
clean-living
clean-cut
clean-up

cleanlier
cleanly → cleanliness
cleanliest

cleaner
cleaned
cleanest
cleaning
cleanable
cleans
cleanness

clean

unclean → uncleanness

uncleanliness

cleanse

cleanses
cleansing
cleanser
cleansed

International Phonetic Alphabet

The table below shows each symbol of the International Phonetic Alphabet (IPA) and provides examples of the associated grapheme(s). The table is not a comprehensive alphabetic code chart; it is intended simply as guidance for teachers in understanding the IPA symbols used in the spelling appendix (English Appendix 1). The pronunciations in the table are, by convention, based on Received Pronunciation and could be significantly different in other accents.

Consonants	
/b/	bad, cabbage
/d/	dog, daddy
/ð/	this
/dʒ/	gem, jug, gauge, judge
/f/	if, puff, photo
/g/	gum, jiggle
/h/	how
/j/	yes
/k/	cat, check, key, school
/l/	leg, hill, kettle
/m/	man, summer, numb
/n/	man, inn, know
/ŋ/	sing, think
/θ/	both
/p/	pet, happy
/r/	red, sorry, wren
/s/	sit, miss, cell, please, notice
/ʃ/	she, chef, cautious, precious
/t/	tea, bottle
/tʃ/	check, fetch
/v/	vet, love
/w/	wet, when
/z/	zip, hens, buzz, tease, xylophone
/ʒ/	pleasure, division, azure

Vowels	
/ɑː/	father, arm
/ɒ/	hot, swan
/æ/	cat
/aɪ/	mind, fine, pie, high, sky, island
/aʊ/	out, cow, bough
/ɛ/	hen, head, said, many
/eɪ/	say, came, bait, weigh
/ɛə/	air, dare, their, prayer
/əʊ/	cold, boat, cone, blow, sew, toe, dough
/ɪ/	hit, England, busy, gym
/ɪə/	beer, ear, here, tier
/iː/	she, bead, see, scheme, chief
/ɔː/	launch, raw, born, ball, fork, poor
/ɔɪ/	coin, boy, buoy
/ʊ/	book, would, wolf, bush
/ʊə/	tour, cure
/uː/	room, you, blue, brute, who, shoe
/ʌ/	cup, monkey, blood, double
/ɜː/	fern, turn, girl, pearl, word
/ə/	farmer, about, dollar

Spelling Journal

In years 2 and 3 you might want to work on 1cm squared maths paper. Using the square to identify phonemes for example:

1.	kn	igh	t		
2.	j	a	ck	e	t
3.	sh	o	ck		

In years 4 - 6 you might want to work in a lined spelling journal. Leave space in between your spells so you can make annotations, spot patterns or provide yourself with learning advice.

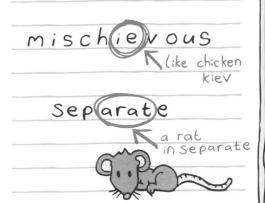

mischievous
like chicken kiev

separate
a rat in separate

- Work in your spelling journal
- Listen to your teacher read the spellings
- Remember to say the word slowly and clearly
- Try your best with your focus five
- Mark your own work and, as you look closer, answer these questions:

1. Which word caused the most difficulty? Why?
2. What was the tricky part?
3. Was it a volatile vowel sound that caused problems?
4. Can you isolate and correct the problem?
5. What have you learnt?
6. How can your spelling get better?

Place any words which are misspelt on The Focus Five Grid. This can be laminated and placed on their desk so everyone is aware of their current spelling challenges. When pupils use any of their focus five accurately they underline with different coloured pens so we can see it being spelt accurately and being used in context.

The Focus Five Grid

The 'Focus Five' grid might be populated from the Go Grapheme Grafters 15 spell check or from analysis of pupils' independent writing. Pupils or teachers can decide which five to focus on.

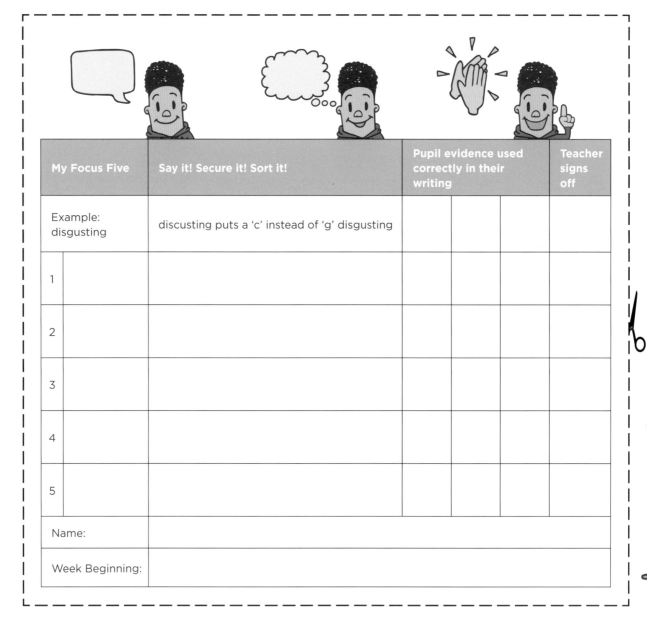

My Focus Five	Say it! Secure it! Sort it!	Pupil evidence used correctly in their writing			Teacher signs off
Example: disgusting	discusting puts a 'c' instead of 'g' disgusting				
1					
2					
3					
4					
5					
Name:					
Week Beginning:					

* Please **photocopy**, **cut out**, **laminate** and **stick** to the pupil's desk.
Once a spelling is used in action accurately it can be replaced with a new targeted spelling.

Investigations & Daily Spelling Experiences

Lens: Good Endings/ Suffixes

GROUPINGS

Investigation 1

30 MINUTES

Hypothesis:

When adding a suffix **-ly** to a word
there are no changes needed to the word

Believe it or not?

Sort and generate a bank of words into the following groups

-ly , -ily, -ally

Do you think the hypothesis is correct?

True 👍	False 👎	Sometimes 👋

Pupil Page

Example Word List:

Teacher introduces some words to develop thinking. Use your professional judgement to introduce words during this investigation to push the learning on.

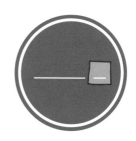

Add -ly to word – NO CHANGE	Word ends in 'y' – drop the 'y' replace with -ily	Word ends in e' – drop the 'e' and add -ly	Words that end in 'ic' – add -ally
kind	happily	gently	basically
friend	angrily	simply	frantically
proper	crazily	humbly	dramatically
actual	extraordinarily	nobly	cynically
eventual	merrily	doubly	automatically
original	hungrily	amply	

Key Learning

☑ **-ly** is a consonant suffix.

☑ If a root word ends in **'e'** then it MUST be dropped before the suffix is added.

☑ If a root work ends in **'y'** then it needs to be dropped and change to **'i'** before the suffix is added.

☑ Do not get confused by words that end in **'ly'** this is not a suffix, e.g. **July**, **only**, **fly**, **family**.

Teacher Support

Lens: Rely on Phonics

Rely on
Phonics

IMPROVING

Go Grapheme Grafters!

Spelling Practice

20 MINUTES

Please note all the words outlined for Year 3 cover focus areas in the National Curriculum.

Focus on these fifteen words on a cycle of two weeks, but go beyond seeing how they cope with the spelling, and target how to remember the tricky parts. This is not to be used as a spelling test. Teach spelling as a problem solving process; a mission to remember spelling for life. In the first instance, show pupils how to combine relying on phonics, then how to use visual and aural emphasis for the difficult bits. Personal problem spellings are identified and targeted through their 'Focus Five'. Encourage your pupils to be 'brave spellers' and to look closely at their mistakes so they can improve, with practice, and commit correct spellings to their long-term memory.

Learning
Look at the sound associations in the word accidentally. If a pupil can spell 'accidentally', then they know that <c> can spell the sound /k/ in the following words: a c cess, a c cessory, su c cess, a c cident, va c cine.
Spell It Out!
Encourage your pupils to spell the words below correctly in their spelling journals. Can they notice that certain sounds appear in other words using the same spellings?

1.	accidentally	6.	angrily	11.	beginning
2.	action	7.	antique	12.	believe
3.	address	8.	anxious	13.	berry
4.	adoration	9.	arrive	14.	bicycle
5.	adventure	10.	beginner	15.	brake

For answers see www.thetrainingspace.co.uk/answers

Lens: Good Endings/ Suffixes

Good Endings/
Suffixes

GROUPINGS

QUICK!

10 MINUTES

Investigate common endings to words. Are they just a common spelling pattern, e.g. **-il** or **-al**? Are they a common ending, e.g. **-tion** or **-cian**?

Can you notice any patterns in the ending?

Learning
Words with endings like /ʒə/ (closure) or /tʃə/ (feature)

Words		
picture	furniture	treasure
measure	nature	pleasure
leisure	enclosure	adventure
creature	disclosure	mixture

Question
Can you notice the pattern in the phonemes and spelling (graphemes)? Can you add any more?

Lens: Good Endings/ Suffixes

Good Endings/ Suffixes

GROUPINGS

STICK!

10 MINUTES

Investigate common endings to words. Are they just a common spelling pattern, e.g. **-il** or **-al**? Are they a common ending, e.g. **-tion** or **-cian**?

Can you notice any patterns in the ending?

Learning
'il' – there are not many words in the English language that end in these two letters

Words		
pencil	email	boil
fossil	unveil	tail
nostril	utensil	tranquil
nail	cocktail	soil

Question
Can you notice how many are nouns?

For answers see www.thetrainingspace.co.uk/answers

Lens: Interrogate and Check

IMPROVING

What a hoot!

FLICK!

10 MINUTES

The owl babies are half asleep and keep making spelling mistakes.
Which letter is wrong? What should it be?

accudent	appeer	dufficult	adnress
e.g. accident	e.g. appear		
actial	brewth	ordenary	theugh
sentre	favourete	complite	busi
occision	appiar	belaeve	reguler
briath	womin	rimember	sertain

Can you find some **spelling errors** in your work and correct them?

Lens: Memorise Rules/Exceptions

Memorise Rules/Exceptions

IMPROVING

Contraction Chaos

 **TICK!**

10 MINUTES

Can you provide the **contracted form** and full forms for each missing part?

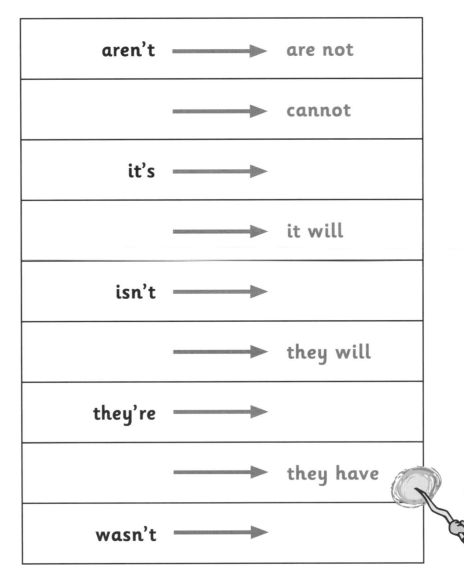

aren't ⟶	are not
⟶	cannot
it's ⟶	
⟶	it will
isn't ⟶	
⟶	they will
they're ⟶	
⟶	they have
wasn't ⟶	

Can you write **3 sentences** for a poster to prevent litter being dropped?
How many **contracted forms** can you include?

For answers see www.thetrainingspace.co.uk/answers

Lens: Pronunciation

Pronunciation

IMPROVING

Post it

 **CLICK!**

10 MINUTES

Can you sort these words so that they are organised into two groups?

Sort in to the /əʊ/ (below) or the /aʊ/ (meow) sound?

slow	grow	anyhow	outgrow	below	flow	know	how
glow	vow	allow	throw	snow	grow	now	mow
eyebrow	meow	blow	wow	borrow	show	brow	highbrow

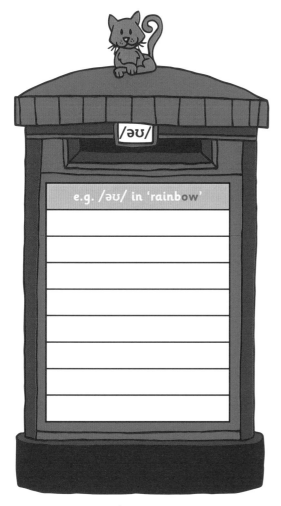

/əʊ/

e.g. /əʊ/ in 'rainbow'

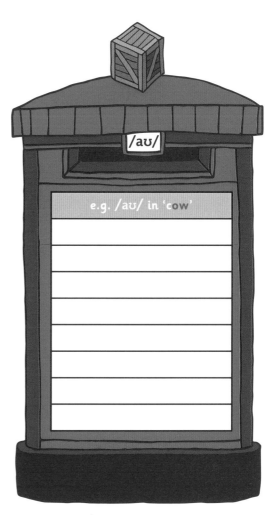

/aʊ/

e.g. /aʊ/ in 'cow'

Lens: Good Endings/ Suffixes

Good Endings/
Suffixes

GROUPINGS

 Investigation 2

30 MINUTES

Hypothesis:

Word can have either **-tion** or **-sion**, added to them.
It does not matter which.

Believe it or not?

Sort and generate a bank of words into the following groups

-tion **or** -sion

Do you think the hypothesis is correct?

True 👍	False 👎	Sometimes 👐

Pupil Page

Example Word List:

Teacher introduces some words to develop thinking. Use your professional judgement to introduce words during this investigation to push the learning on.

		Words that end in -tion	Words that end in -sion
inflate	transfuse	navigation	decision
conserve	navigate	inflation	extension
vibrate	televise	qualification	collision
decide	conclude	vibration	television
confuse	pronounce	dictation	supervision
tempt	variety	temptation	corrosion
corrode	collide	conservation	conclusion
educate	extend	pronunciation	explosion
expect	create	communication	confusion
divide	punctuate	education	

Key Learning

☑ The suffix **-tion** and **-sion** sound the same and cause many spelling problems.

☑ If the word is related to one that ends in **'d'**, or **'se'**, then the suffix is **-sion**.

☑ If the noun is related to a word ending in **'ate'** then it is **-tion**.

Lens: Rely on Phonics

Rely on
Phonics

IMPROVING

Go Grapheme Grafters!

Spelling Practice

20 MINUTES

Please note all the words outlined for Year 3 cover focus areas in the National Curriculum.

Focus on these fifteen words on a cycle of two weeks, but go beyond seeing how they cope with the spelling, and target how to remember the tricky parts. This is not to be used as a spelling test. Teach spelling as a problem solving process; a mission to remember spelling for life. In the first instance, show pupils how to combine relying on phonics, then how to use visual and aural emphasis for the difficult bits. Personal problem spellings are identified and targeted through their 'Focus Five'. Encourage your pupils to be 'brave spellers' and to look closely at their mistakes so they can improve, with practice, and commit correct spellings to their long-term memory.

Learning
Look at the sound associations in the word break. If a pupil can spell 'break', then they know that <ea> can spell the sound /eɪ/ in the following words: great, steak, breaker , greater, greatest.

Spell It Out!
Encourage your pupils to spell the words below correctly in their spelling journals. Can they notice that certain sounds appear in other words using the same spellings?

1.	break	6.	century	11.	chorus
2.	brochure	7.	chalet	12.	circle
3.	build	8.	character	13.	closure
4.	bury	9.	chef	14.	collision
5.	calendar	10.	chemist	15.	commission

For answers see www.thetrainingspace.co.uk/answers

Lens: Good Endings/ Suffixes

Good Endings/ Suffixes

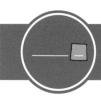

GROUPINGS

QUICK!

10 MINUTES

Investigate common endings to words. Are they just a common spelling pattern, e.g. **-il** or **-al**? Are they a common ending, e.g. **-tion** or **-cian**?

Can you notice any patterns in the ending?

Learning
If the ending sounds like /ʒən/ it is spelt as -sion.
Question
Can you sort into good and bad spelling?
Words

invacian	televician
confusion	division
collician	decision

Lens: Recognising Punctuation

STICK!

10 MINUTES

Knowing the types of punctuation that are used within words, e.g. **apostrophes** and **hyphens**. Understanding the function of these punctuation marks ensures proper usage.

Learning
Apostrophes are used to show omitted letters when two words are contracted together.

Words	
couldn't	you're
hadn't	shouldn't
we're	we'll
wouldn't	we've
hasn't	weren't
you'll	shan't

Question
Can you identify the negative contractions in this list?

For answers see www.thetrainingspace.co.uk/answers

Lens: Rely on Phonics

Rely on
Phonics

IMPROVING

Phoneme Finders

10 MINUTES

Find the long vowel sound /aɪ/ as in mind, fine, pie, try

Tike liked to ride his bike. He had an invite from his friend Mike who asked him if he minded going to the park to go on an adventure.

Tike loved to go out on dry, fine days and look at the sky and ride high up the hills. He also liked to collect pine cones and wild items from nature.

They headed off for the ride and enjoyed spying all the beautiful things that reminded them of autumn. When they got home Mum had made a pear pie!

	Collect all the words with this sound					
Grapheme	i	i-e	ie	igh	y	is
Examples found						

Which were the most common ways to represent the long vowel sound /aɪ/?

For answers see www.thetrainingspace.co.uk/answers

Lens: Order of Letters

Order of
Letters

qu

IMPROVING

Find Your Team

TICK!

10 MINUTES

Can you sort the words into the correct group?

Learning
pencil   uncle   cycle   audience   century   unicycle   monocle   parcel   cancel
recycle   silence   centre   icicle   stencil   exciting   bicycle   miracle
particle   necessary   circle   excellent   notice   council   motorcycle

Word Wizard	Fairy Spell Mother	Fred the Frog
Soft 'c' inc in the word sounds like 's'	'hard c' inc in the word sounds like 'k'	Includes soft and hard 'c'
pencil	uncle	cycle

For answers see www.thetrainingspace.co.uk/answers

Lens: Verification

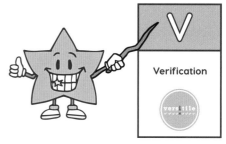

Verification

IMPROVING

Good Spells Vs Bad Spells?

 CLICK! 10 MINUTES

Can you sort this list into correct spellings and incorrect spellings?
Can you rewrite the incorrect spellings accurately?

Learning				
through	womun	lenth	potatos	grammar
positsion	experience	suppose	centre	height
thought	therefore	discide	ordinary	notise
famus	appear	gard	early	island

Correct	Incorrect
through	womun ➡ woman

Lens: Recognising Punctuation

R

Recognising Punctuation

GROUPINGS

Investigation 3

30 MINUTES

Hypothesis:

The **apostrophe** in a contracted form always represents **one omitted letter**.

Believe it or not?

How many can pupils generate by themselves?

Do you think the hypothesis is correct?

True 👍	False 👎	Sometimes 👐

Pupil Page

Example Word List:

Teacher introduces some words to develop thinking. Use your professional judgement to introduce words during this investigation to push the learning on.

Expanded Form		Contracted Form	
do not	she is/has		
cannot	he is/has		
is not	it is/has		
does not	there is/has		
will not			
I had			
I would			
I have			
I will			
I am			

Key Learning

☑ **Apostrophes** are used where two words have been joined and some letters missed out so that a **contraction** is formed.

☑ Be careful of the homophone issue, **its/it's**, **there's/theirs**.

☑ Contractions occur more in **dialogue** or **informal styles**.

Lens: Rely on Phonics

Rely on Phonics

IMPROVING

Go Grapheme Grafters!

 Spelling Practice

20 MINUTES

Please note all the words outlined for Year 3 cover focus areas in the National Curriculum.

Focus on these fifteen words on a cycle of two weeks, but go beyond seeing how they cope with the spelling, and target how to remember the tricky parts. This is not to be used as a spelling test. Teach spelling as a problem solving process; a mission to remember spelling for life. In the first instance, show pupils how to combine relying on phonics, then how to use visual and aural emphasis for the difficult bits. Personal problem spellings are identified and targeted through their 'Focus Five'. Encourage your pupils to be 'brave spellers' and to look closely at their mistakes so they can improve, with practice, and commit correct spellings to their long-term memory.

Learning
Look at the sound associations in the word complete. If a pupil can spell 'complete', then they know that <e_e> can spell the sound /iː/ in the following words: theme, these, concrete, compete, delete.

Spell It Out!
Encourage your pupils to spell the words below correctly in their spelling journals. Can they notice that certain sounds appear in other words using the same spellings?

1.	complete	6.	describe	11.	division
2.	completion	7.	different	12.	double
3.	confusion	8.	disappear	13.	early
4.	continue	9.	disappoint	14.	earth
5.	decision	10.	discipline	15.	echo

For answers see www.thetrainingspace.co.uk/answers

Lens: Recognising Punctuation

Recognising Punctuation

GROUPINGS

QUICK!

10 MINUTES

Knowing the types of punctuation that are used within words, e.g. **apostrophes** and **hyphens**. Understanding the function of these punctuation marks ensures proper usage.

Learning
Two words are contracted together to make the contracted form. An apostrophe shows omitted letters.

Question
Can you turn these two words into contracted form? Can you add anymore? Sort into positive and negative.

Words	
could not	I will
has not	should not
we will	I am
you have	who are
we are	he will

Lens: **Prefixes**

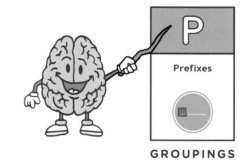

P

Prefixes

GROUPINGS

STICK!

10 MINUTES

Understanding prefixes will mean pupils will learn the general principles for applying them. Certain prefixes hold meaning and they can support their spelling and vocabulary extension.

Learning			
The prefix dis- means reversing and un- means not.			
Words			
kind	unkind	like	dislike
agree		honest	
order		popular	
tidy		please	
trust		lucky	
friendly		comfort	
fair		well	
Question			
Can you add dis- or un- to create the opposite negative meaning?			

Lens: Inspecting a Dictionary

IMPROVING

Dictionary Disaster

FLICK!

10 MINUTES

What a disaster! The words keep changing position.
Help the Word Wizard put them in **alphabetical order**.

Jumbled Order	Dictionary Order 1	Jumbled Order	Dictionary Order 2
1. relative	1.	1. merit	1.
2. register	2.	2. message	2.
3. reign	3.	3. mercury	3.
4. release	4.	4. metallic	4.
5. regular	5.	5. mention	5.

Jumbled Order	Dictionary Order 3	Jumbled Order	Dictionary Order 4
1. potato	1.	1. imprison	1.
2. possible	2.	2. important	2.
3. postage	3.	3. improve	3.
4. potential	4.	4. impractical	4.
5. posture	5.	5. impress	5.

Can you design a list of five words for your friend to re-order?

For answers see www.thetrainingspace.co.uk/answers

P48

Lens: Navigating a Thesaurus

N

Navigating
a Thesaurus

Red

IMPROVING

Synonym Spectacular

Red

TICK!

10 MINUTES

Can you add in the missing letters for the words
in the same **synonym family**?

Sleep	d r _ _ _ ⟶ d r e a m
	1. s l _ _ _ e r 5. _ _ d
	2. _ _ _ t i m e 6. r _ _ t
	3. _ _ z _ 7. _ _ _ _ e y e
	4. n _ _ 8. s n _ _ _ _
Run	b r _ _ k ⟶ b r e a k
	1. r _ _ _ 5. d _ _ t
	2. _ _ s h 6. _ _ s h
	3. s p u _ _ 7. _ _ g
	4. _ _ _ _ n t 8. e s c _ _ e
Tall	_ _ _ k y ⟶ l a n k y
	1. s _ _ r i n g 5. g _ _ _ t
	2. t _ w e r _ _ _ 6. l _ _ t y
	3. h _ _ h 7. s k y s c _ _ _ _ _ _
	4. e l e _ _ _ e d 8. s i z a _ _ _
Dark	c l _ _ _ _ ⟶ c l o u d y
	1. _ _ m 5. g l _ _ _ y
	2. d _ _ g y 6. m _ _ k _
	3. d _ _ b 7. s h _ _ _ _ y
	4. _ _ l l 8. d _ _ k y

Can you use a **thesaurus** to add more?

For answers see www.thetrainingspace.co.uk/answers

Lens: Guesses

Spells & Smells & Potions & Notions!

CLICK!

10 MINUTES

In pairs take turns. One of your pair will have the answers ready, whilst the other one has to work out the hidden word.

Can you correctly find the word within **ten guesses**? Each wrong letter guess adds a spoonful of liquid.

Make sure the potion doesn't **explode**.

Definition	Letters	Amount of guesses					
An exciting experience	a d _ _ _ _ _ _ _	1 2 3 4 5 6 7 8 9 10					
An unwelcome intrusion into someone else's place	i n _ _ s _ _ _	1 2 3 4 5 6 7 8 9 10					
Two moving objects crashing together	c _ l l _ _ _ o n	1 2 3 4 5 6 7 8 9 10					
A substance that can cause harm	p _ _ _ _ n	1 2 3 4 5 6 7 8 9 10					
An elegant woman	g l _ m _ r _ _ _	1 2 3 4 5 6 7 8 9 10					
A very brave person	c o _ _ _ _ _ _ u s	1 2 3 4 5 6 7 8 9 10					
Sudden impulse	u n _ x _ _ _ _ _ _	1 2 3 4 5 6 7 8 9 10					

Lens: Recognising Punctuation

Recognising Punctuation

GROUPINGS

 Investigation 4

30 MINUTES

Hypothesis:

The most common **contracted form** is one omitted letter with one **apostrophe** used in its place.

Believe it or not?

How many can pupils generate by themselves?

One omitted letter = one apostrophe	Two or more omitted letters – one apostrophe	Other contractions

Do you think the hypothesis is correct?

True 👍	False 👎	Sometimes

Pupil Page

Example Word List:

Teacher introduces some words to develop thinking. Use your professional judgement to introduce words during this investigation to push the learning on.

he's	I'd	won't
you're	can't	we'd
they've	I've	he'd
I'm	aren't	you'd
she'd	weren't	I'll
couldn't	he'll	she's
shan't	you've	we're
they're	they'd	she'll
they'll	haven't	we've
we'll	you'll	they'll

Key Learning

☑ In Shakespeare's time all omitted letters were shown by **apostrophes**.

☑ **Won't** and **shan't** are unusual because the base words have been modified.

☑ **Contracted form** is used in more informal writing.

Lens: Rely on Phonics

Go Grapheme Grafters!

Spelling Practice

20 MINUTES

Please note all the words outlined for Year 3 cover focus areas in the National Curriculum.

Focus on these fifteen words on a cycle of two weeks, but go beyond seeing how they cope with the spelling, and target how to remember the tricky parts. This is not to be used as a spelling test. Teach spelling as a problem solving process; a mission to remember spelling for life. In the first instance, show pupils how to combine relying on phonics, then how to use visual and aural emphasis for the difficult bits. Personal problem spellings are identified and targeted through their 'Focus Five'. Encourage your pupils to be 'brave spellers' and to look closely at their mistakes so they can improve, with practice, and commit correct spellings to their long-term memory.

Learning
Look at the sound associations in the word Egypt. If a pupil can spell 'Egypt', then they know that <y> can spell the sound /ɪ/ in the following words: gym, myth, symbol, pyramid, mystery.

Spell It Out!
Encourage your pupils to spell the words below correctly in their spelling journals. Can they notice that certain sounds appear in other words using the same spellings?

1.	Egypt	6.	famous	11.	gently
7.	eight	7.	fare	12.	grate
3.	exercise	8.	fascinate	13.	great
4.	expression	9.	forgetting	14.	gym
5.	fair	10.	forgotten	15.	happily

For answers see www.thetrainingspace.co.uk/answers

Lens: Recognising Punctuation

Recognising Punctuation

GROUPINGS

 QUICK!

10 MINUTES

Knowing the types of punctuation that are used within words, e.g. **apostrophes** and **hyphens**. Understanding the function of these punctuation marks ensures proper usage. These two are different.

Learning
Show that something belongs to someone by putting an apostrophe before the -s (singular).

Words	
the teacher	dog
Ben	book
Sophie	hat
the dog	coat
the girl	bowl
the boy	lead

Question
Can you pair these people with their objects/pets?

Lens: Irregular/ Exception Words

Irregular/ Exception Words

GROUPINGS

STICK!

10 MINUTES

Set 2

Certain words do not follow patterns and these could be for phonetic reasons or systems for pluralising. There are irregular words that need to be learnt.

Learning
These are unusual spellings **and high frequency in English.**

Words			
could	should	around	move
prove	improve	most	only
both	clothes	every	everybody
any	many	busy	money
pretty	again	about	because
beautiful	even	parents	people
sugar	sure	water	eye
hour	who	where	Christmas

Question
Can you learn these words perfectly?

For answers see www.thetrainingspace.co.uk/answers

Lens: Check Etymology

Check
Etymology

ACQUIRING

Etymology Ladders

FLICK!

10 MINUTES

Pattern Climber

All of these words have a component that means the **same thing**.
Can you identify the **word** and the **meaning** of the **component**?

Hint: All definitions mention **moving people**, **objects** or **information** in the clue.

Clue	Answer contains the word 'port'
1. Carries luggage to help new visitors at a hotel	
2. To carry goods out of one country to sell to another	
3. When one nation carries goods from another nation	
4. Many goods are movable and easy to carry	
5. Focus on the crucial concerns that need communicating	
6. Reporters do this when they carry information to the public	
7. Human beings can be legally removed from one country	
8. The vehicles that are used for goods and people to be carried	

Lens: **Analogies**

Analogies

ACQUIRING

Conjure a Word Storm

e.g. could would should

TICK!

10 MINUTES

Can you change **one sound** (one letter or two letters) to create a new word?
You must bring it back to the word that starts the circle.

Using the letters below, start with **one word** and change **one letter** or digraph (two letters) to make a new word. See if you can find a word for each box to complete the circle.

s, l, c, f, i, a, p, ck, b

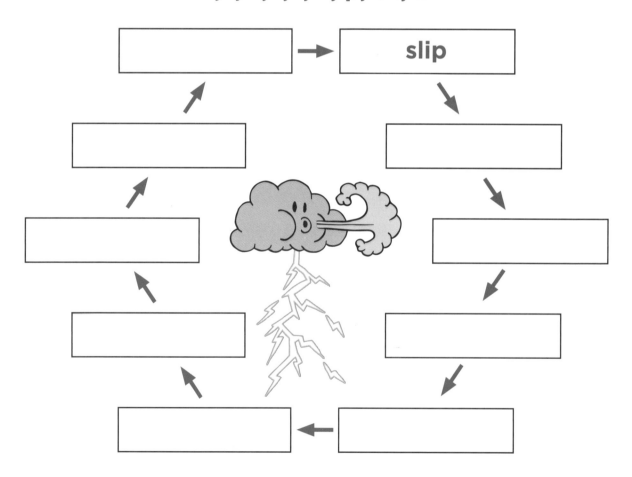

slip

You can only use a word once

For answers see www.thetrainingspace.co.uk/answers

Lens: Noticing Families and Roots

N

Noticing Families and Roots

ACQUIRING

Build the Spell

CLICK!

10 MINUTES

How many new words can you build using the **prefixes** and **suffixes**?

Prefixes*		LEARNING You might need to drop or change or add letters when adding a suffix.	Suffixes*	
Means	**Examples**		**Examples**	**Means**
Apart	dis- dif- di-		-ful -ous -ious	Much/ Full of/ Fill
Not/ Opposite	non- un- im- in- il- ir-	**cover**	-ship	Position held
			-sion -tion	State of being
		logic	-ic -ial	Having the form
			-ive	Nature of
With/ Together	co- com- con-		-ment	Condition
			-ness	Quality
Cause to	em- en-	**part**	-ance -ence	State
Again	re-		-ing	Action
Against	anti-	**home**	-ery	Place of Work
Reverse/ Remove	de-		-age	Result
Wrongly	mis-	**behave**	-ible -able	Ability
			-ish	Little
Before	fore-		-ly	Characteristic
Between	inter-		-y	Without

Challenge: Can you try new combinations with your own root or base words?

*This is not an exhaustive list

Lens: Organising Sounds

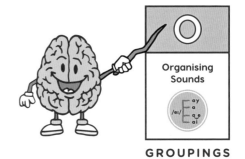

GROUPINGS

Investigation 5

30 MINUTES

Hypothesis:

The least common graphemes to represent the /eɪ/ sounds are 'ei', 'eigh' or 'ey'.

Believe it or not?

Common	Rare	
ay	ea	aigh
ai	ei	eigh
a-e	e-e	ey

Do you think the hypothesis is correct?

True 👍	False 👎	Sometimes 〰️

Pupil Page

Example Word List:

Teacher introduces some words to develop thinking. Use your professional judgement to introduce words during this investigation to push the learning on.

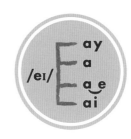

rain	pane	eight
fete	pain	neighbour
vein	weigh	obey
say	whey	prey
day	may	tray
they	train	wait
straight	late	snake
lane	bake	mate
great	brain	play

Key Learning

☑ There are many ways to represent the phoneme /eɪ/.

☑ Some are more common and are present in more words.

☑ Some spelling patterns are rare but in common words, e.g. they.

Lens: Rely on Phonics

Rely on
Phonics

IMPROVING

Go Grapheme Grafters!

Spelling Practice

20 MINUTES

Please note all the words outlined for Year 3 cover focus areas in the National Curriculum.

Focus on these fifteen words on a cycle of two weeks, but go beyond seeing how they cope with the spelling, and target how to remember the tricky parts. This is not to be used as a spelling test. Teach spelling as a problem solving process; a mission to remember spelling for life. In the first instance, show pupils how to combine relying on phonics, then how to use visual and aural emphasis for the difficult bits. Personal problem spellings are identified and targeted through their 'Focus Five'. Encourage your pupils to be 'brave spellers' and to look closely at their mistakes so they can improve, with practice, and commit correct spellings to their long-term memory.

Learning
Look at the sound associations in the word hesitation. **If a pupil can spell 'hesitation', then they know that** <s> **can spell the sound** /z/ **in the following words: cou_s_in, hu_s_band, bu_s_iness, sea_s_on, becau_s_e.**

Spell It Out!
Encourage your pupils to spell the words below correctly in their spelling journals. Can they notice that certain sounds appear in other words using the same spellings?

1.	hesitation	6.	immature	11.	invasion
2.	hideous	7.	incorrect	12.	invention
3.	humbly	8.	information	13.	irregular
4.	humorous	9.	injection	14.	league
5.	illegal	10.	interact	15.	machine

For answers see www.thetrainingspace.co.uk/answers

Lens: Organising Sounds

QUICK!

10 MINUTES

Listening carefully to phonemes and syllables. Knowing there are good phonic and letter string guesses for common sounds. Learning how to make the most plausible choices.

Learning
The letter string 'ch' is commonly sounded as /k/ (as in 'school') or /tʃ/ (as in 'snatch'). Less commonly, this can be sounded as /ʃ/ (as in 'crochet'). Words that contain the /ʃ/ sound to represent the letter string 'ch' often come from French words.

Words	
scheme	chemist
chef	echo
chorus	brochure
witch	machine
character	church

Question
Can you sort these words into their different sounds for 'ch'?   'ch' sounds like /ʃ/ 'sh'

Lens: Irregular/ Exception Words

Irregular/ Exception Words

GROUPINGS

STICK!

🕐 **10 MINUTES**

Certain words do not follow patterns and these could be for phonetic reasons or systems for pluralising. There are irregular words that need to be learnt.

Learning
These are unusual spellings **and** high frequency **in English.**

Words				
door	floor	poor	old	gold
cold	told	great	break	steak
fried	kind	mind	behind	climb
child	children	wild	fast	last
past	after	path	bath	class
pass	grass	future	plant	half

Question
Can you learn these words perfectly? Can you test and support your friends?

For answers see www.thetrainingspace.co.uk/answers

Lens: Understanding Patterns

Understanding Patterns

ACQUIRING

Spell Maker

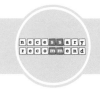  

These words have become disordered when the spell went wrong.
Please rebuild correctly.

Jumbled Order	Correct order
e.g. act re tion	**reaction**
able live un	
able sell re	
ing un cover	
ful dis respect	
heat ed re	
lock un able	
ing pre view	
heat ing pre	
ment place re	

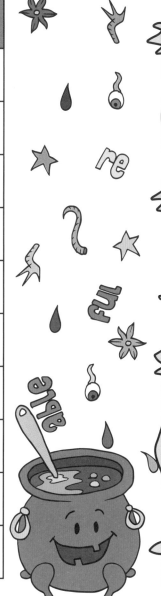

Lens: I/Me Personal Spelling

ACQUIRING

My Focus Five

 **TICK!**

Personal Spells I Need to Target!

10 MINUTES

This information might come from Go Grapheme Grafters or from analysis of independent writing. Pupils or teachers can decide the five to target.

My Focus Five	Say it! Secure it! Sort it!	Pupil evidence used correctly in their writing			Teacher signs off
Example: disgusting	discusting puts a 'c' instead of 'g' disgusting				
1					
2					
3					
4					
5					
Name:					
Week Beginning:					

For answers see www.thetrainingspace.co.uk/answers

Lens: Recognising Parts

Recognising Parts

ACQUIRING

Broom Zoom!

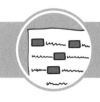

CLICK!

10 MINUTES

Izzy Whizzy! Let's get busy!

Two brooms can crash together to make one word.

-ion or -ian

Do you need to add and -ion or -ian to the ending?

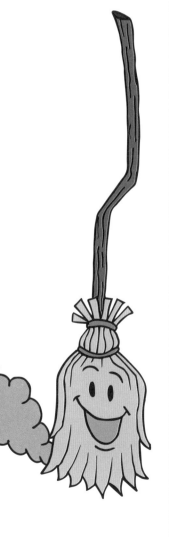

invent →	invention
music →	musician
magic	
inject	
express	
act	
electric	
confess	
discuss	
mathematic	

Lens: Organising Sounds

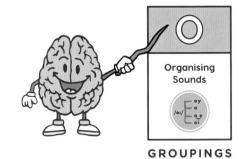

Organising
Sounds

GROUPINGS

Investigation 6

30 MINUTES

Hypothesis:

All words that included the phoneme 'ch'
sounds like the 'ch' in charmed.

Believe it or not?

How many can pupils generate by themselves?

'ch'	'k'
The 'ch' in the word sounds like the 'ch' in charmed	The 'ch' in the word sounds like the 'ch' in chaos

Do you think the hypothesis is correct?

True 👍	False 👎	Sometimes 🖐️

Pupil Page

Example Word List:

Teacher introduces some words to develop thinking. Use your professional judgement to introduce words during this investigation to push the learning on.

champion	sandwich	chloride
lunch	chorus	change
chrome	scheme	stomach
tech	watch	witch
chips	chemist	chirp
monarch	character	chair
teach	chemical	cherries

Key Learning

☑ 'ch' represents three phonemes /tʃ/ as in champion, /k/ as in tech and /ʃ/ as in chef.

☑ The /k/ and /ʃ/ are much less common.

Lens: Rely on Phonics

Rely on
Phonics

IMPROVING

Go Grapheme Grafters!

 Spelling Practice

20 MINUTES

Please note all the words outlined for Year 3 cover focus areas in the National Curriculum.

Focus on these fifteen words on a cycle of two weeks, but go beyond seeing how they cope with the spelling, and target how to remember the tricky parts. This is not to be used as a spelling test. Teach spelling as a problem solving process; a mission to remember spelling for life. In the first instance, show pupils how to combine relying on phonics, then how to use visual and aural emphasis for the difficult bits. Personal problem spellings are identified and targeted through their 'Focus Five'. Encourage your pupils to be 'brave spellers' and to look closely at their mistakes so they can improve, with practice, and commit correct spellings to their long-term memory.

Learning
Look at the sound associations in the word measure. If a pupil can spell 'measure', then they know that <s> can spell the sound /ʒ/ in the following words: trea_s_ure, plea_s_ure, enclo_s_ure, clo_s_ure, lei_s_ure.

Spell It Out!
Encourage your pupils to spell the words below correctly in their spelling journals. Can they notice that certain sounds appear in other words using the same spellings?

1.	measure	6.	nobly	11.	science
2.	misbehave	7.	picture	12.	sensation
3.	myth	8.	prefer	13.	serious
4.	nature	9.	scene	14.	simply
5.	neighbour	10.	scheme	15.	subheading

For answers see www.thetrainingspace.co.uk/answers

Lens: Organising Sounds

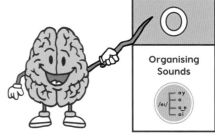

QUICK!

10 MINUTES

Listening carefully to phonemes and syllables. Knowing there are good phonic and letter string guesses for common sounds. Learning how to make the most plausible choices.

Learning
Words with the /ʃ/ sound spelt 'ch' are mostly of French origin.

Words	
chef	chiffon
Charlotte	machine
chandelier	parachute
chalet	chevron
champagne	brochure

Question
Can you notice the sound that the 'ch' is making?

Lens: New Meaning/ Homophone

New Meaning/ Homophone

GROUPINGS

Compound Words

STICK!

10 MINUTES

Compound words are two words in their own right that join and make a new word. There is often an associated meaning.

Learning
These are called closed compound words. No space between them.

Words

Long vowel /ʊə/ (fallout)   Long vowel /ɛə/ (airliner)
Long vowel /ɪə/ (deerstalker)

talkback	hairbrush	clearway	flyover	wheelchair
walkway	spearmint	underwear	frogspawn	upstairs
yearbook	hallmark	freefall	warlike	cheerleader
seesaw	waterfall	ballpark	downstairs	therefore

Question

Can you sort these compound words into the correct long vowel categories? /ʊə/ /ɛə/ or /ɪə/?
Or words that do not include any of these vowel sounds?

For answers see www.thetrainingspace.co.uk/answers

Lens: Illustrative

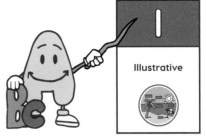

Illustrative

ACQUIRING

Themed Words

FLICK!

10 MINUTES

The Toy Shop

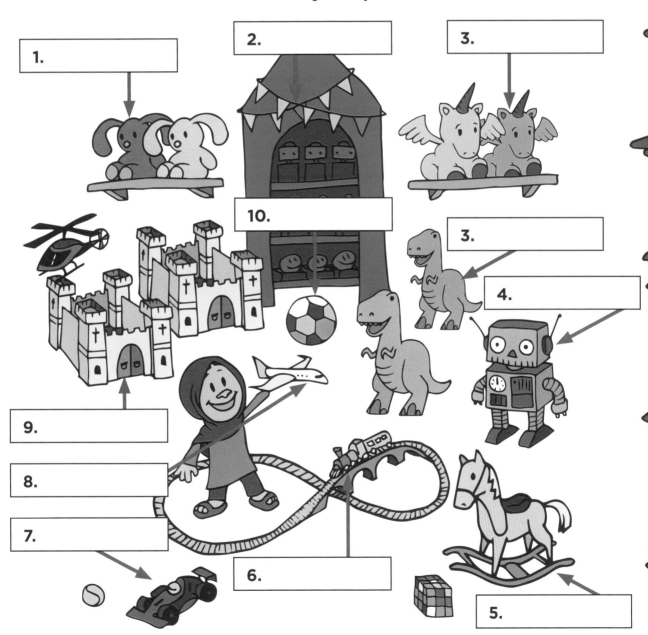

1.

2.

3.

10.

3.

4.

9.

8.

7.

6.

5.

Can you label this picture with accurately spelt words?
Can you draw your own picture and label it?

Lens: Noticing Families and Roots

ACQUIRING

Flying Families

 **TICK!**

10 MINUTES

Can the baby owls pair up words that **sound the same** but **mean different things**?

A good pair is a **homophone** or **near homophone**.

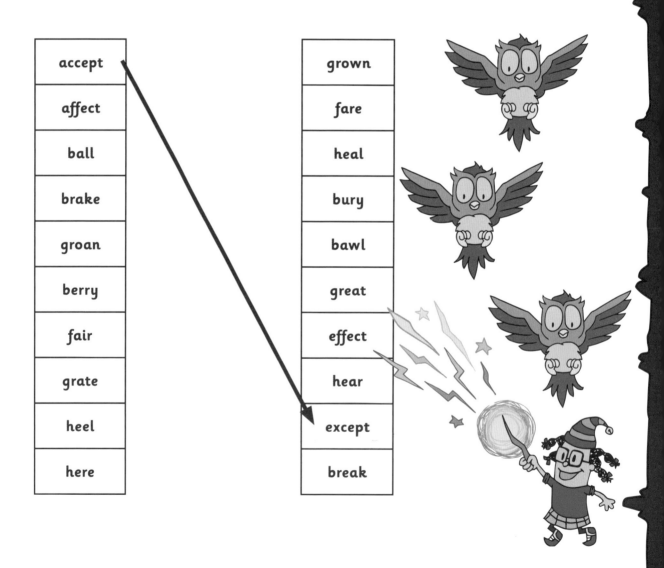

accept	grown
affect	fare
ball	heal
brake	bury
groan	bawl
berry	great
fair	effect
grate	hear
heel	except
here	break

Can you define and explain the difference between the two?

For answers see www.thetrainingspace.co.uk/answers

Lens: Go! Speed! Write!

ACQUIRING

Midnight Mayhem

CLICK!

10 MINUTES

Race home before midnight otherwise your clothes will turn to rags and your transport will turn into a pumpkin. You have **5 minutes.**

- Work in pairs.
- Put 5 minutes on a timer.
- Your friend reads sentences from a book slowly and calmly. They can choose the book.
- They read it as many times as you need (a sentence at a time).
- You write down the dictated sentences.
- Together, analyse spelling mistakes and help each other improve.
- You then swap and repeat.

Write your sentences below

Lens: Understanding Plurals

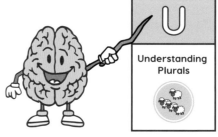

GROUPINGS

Investigation 7

30 MINUTES

Hypothesis:

When making a plural just add -s, However you need to add -es after words ending in 'y', 's(s)', 'ch', 'sh', 'z(z)' and when 'y' is replaced with 'i'.

Believe it or not?

How many can pupils generate by themselves?

Do you think the hypothesis is correct?

True 👍	False 👎	Sometimes 🖐

Pupil Page

Example Word List:

Teacher introduces some words to develop thinking. Use your professional judgement to introduce words during this investigation to push the learning on.

s(s)	z(z)	x	sh	ch	y
bus	buzz	fox	crash	church	lolly
buses	buzzes	foxes	crashes	churches	lollies
		box	rush	bench	lorry
		boxes	rushes	benches	lorries
				beach	fly
				beaches	flies
				catch	party
				catches	parties

Key Learning

☑ When adding -s and -es to nouns and verbs, simply add an -s to the base word unless they have the endings above.

☑ Note if a word ends in 'f' or 'fe' then they need to be replaced with a 'v' then -es added.

Teacher Support

Lens: Rely on Phonics

R
Rely on Phonics

IMPROVING

Go Grapheme Grafters!

Spelling Practice

20 MINUTES

Please note all the words outlined for Year 3 cover focus areas in the National Curriculum.

Focus on these fifteen words on a cycle of two weeks, but go beyond seeing how they cope with the spelling, and target how to remember the tricky parts. This is not to be used as a spelling test. Teach spelling as a problem solving process; a mission to remember spelling for life. In the first instance, show pupils how to combine relying on phonics, then how to use visual and aural emphasis for the difficult bits. Personal problem spellings are identified and targeted through their 'Focus Five'. Encourage your pupils to be 'brave spellers' and to look closely at their mistakes so they can improve, with practice, and commit correct spellings to their long-term memory.

Learning
Look at the sound associations in the word television. If a pupil can spell 'television', then they know that <si> can spell the sound /ʒ/ in the following words: division, invasion, decision, confusion, collision.

Spell It Out!
Encourage your pupils to spell the words below correctly in their spelling journals. Can they notice that certain sounds appear in other words using the same spellings?

1.	television	6.	trouble	11.	about
2.	they	7.	various	12.	abruptly
3.	tongue	8.	vein	13.	accidentally
4.	touch	9.	weigh	14.	account
5.	treasure	10.	young	15.	ache

For answers see www.thetrainingspace.co.uk/answers

Lens: Understanding Plurals

GROUPINGS

QUICK!

10 MINUTES

Plurals are a big area of understanding. Most singular nouns form the plural by adding –s, e.g. boat to boats, house to houses.

However, if the singular noun ends in 's', 'x', 'ch' or 'sh' you make a plural by adding -es, e.g. bus to buses and pitch to pitches. If the singular noun ends in 'y' then this is dropped and replaced with –ies, e.g. penny to pennies.

However, there are also some irregular noun plurals, e.g. woman to women, child to children, mouse to mice. To make it even harder, some plurals are the same in the singular form, e.g. sheep, fish, species, aircraft.

Learning
Words that end in 'y' drop the 'y' and replace with 'i' before adding 'e' to make plural.

Words	
babys – babies	storys – stories
familys – families	memorys – memories
bodys – bodies	butterflys - butterflies

Question
Can you choose the correctly spelt word?

Lens: Understanding Plurals

Understanding
Plurals

GROUPINGS

STICK!

🕙 10 MINUTES

Plurals are a big area of understanding. Most singular nouns form the plural by adding –s, e.g. boat to boats, house to houses.

However, if the singular noun ends in 's', 'x', 'ch' or 'sh' you make a plural by adding -es, e.g. bus to buses and pitch to pitches. If the singular noun ends in 'y' then this is dropped and replaced with –ies, e.g. penny to pennies.

However, there are also some irregular noun plurals, e.g. woman to women, child to children, mouse to mice. To make it even harder, some plurals are the same in the singular form, e.g. sheep, fish, species, aircraft.

Learning			
Words that end with 's', 'x', 'z', 'ch' or 'sh' require -es.			
Words			
box	crash	bus	glass
waltz	beach	pitch	dish
church	wish	fox	watch
desk	ruler	door	ring
pencil	house	cloud	book
dry	pen	cat	cup
Question			
Can you pluralise these words? Can you notice why some words need -es?			

Lens: Interrogate and Check

IMPROVING

Spot the Spells

FLICK!

10 MINUTES

Can you find the **10 spelling errors** in this piece of work and edit it to the correct **spellings**?

Dear Diary,

Today in the library, I found some new matariel from my favorite author. I was considerring reading a diferent author's work, that I herd good things about and I know they are populur. Imagiine my face when the librariun told me that a specal delivery had arrived.... A book by my favourote writer.

(10 Errors)

---

1. ☐   4. ☐   7. ☐   10. ☐

2. ☐   5. ☐   8. ☐

3. ☐   6. ☐   9. ☐

Lens: Memorise Rules/Exceptions

Memorise Rules/Exceptions

IMPROVING

Magic Mix Up

TICK!

10 MINUTES

These objects have been **jumbled up** with their owners.
Can you pair the **owner** to **their object?** Add the **apostrophe** in the correct place.

10 people / animals	10 objects	
girls	bikes	girls' school
boys	handbags	
babies	house	
men	school	
children	food	
mice	population	
dogs	cheese	
chickens	bowls	
Cyprus	sweets	
teachers	marking	

For answers see www.thetrainingspace.co.uk/answers

Lens: Pronunciation

Pronunciation

IMPROVING

Hocus Pocus Rhyme Time

10 MINUTES

Can you generate one syllable and multisyllable words that rhyme with these words?
Can you sort them into the correct group/letter representaion for that sound?

1. Learn

urn	earn	ern	other
burn	yearn	fern	adjourn

2. May

ay	ey	eigh	other
slay	grey	sleigh	ballet

3. Reign

ane	aign	ain	other
mane	campaign	brain	vein

Lens: Understanding Plurals

Understanding Plurals

GROUPINGS

Investigation 8

30 MINUTES

Hypothesis:

Not all words that end in 'f' or 'fe' have a letter/letters dropped and replaced with 'v' before adding in -es for the plural form.

Believe it or not?

How many can pupils generate by themselves?

Do you think the hypothesis is correct?

True 👍	False 👎	Sometimes 🖐

Pupil Page

Example Word List:

Teacher introduces some words to develop thinking. Use your professional judgement to introduce words during this investigation to push the learning on.

calf	leaf
half	life
hoof	loaf
knife	scarf
shelf	cliff
wife	chief
wolf	giraffe
thief	belief
chef	ref

Key Learning

☑ Nouns that end with 'f' or 'fe' change 'f' or 'fe' to 'v' then add -es.

☑ There are a few exceptions to this rule, e.g. giraffes, beliefs, chefs.

Teacher Support

Lens: Rely on Phonics

Rely on Phonics

IMPROVING

Go Grapheme Grafters!

 Spelling Practice 🕐 20 MINUTES

Please note all the words outlined for Year 3 cover focus areas in the National Curriculum.

Focus on these fifteen words on a cycle of two weeks, but go beyond seeing how they cope with the spelling, and target how to remember the tricky parts. This is not to be used as a spelling test. Teach spelling as a problem solving process; a mission to remember spelling for life. In the first instance, show pupils how to combine relying on phonics, then how to use visual and aural emphasis for the difficult bits. Personal problem spellings are identified and targeted through their 'Focus Five'. Encourage your pupils to be 'brave spellers' and to look closely at their mistakes so they can improve, with practice, and commit correct spellings to their long-term memory.

Learning
Look at the sound associations in the word admiration. If a pupil can spell 'admiration', then they know that <ti> can spell the sound /ʃ/ in the following words: information, adoration, sensation, preparation, donation.

Spell It Out!
Encourage your pupils to spell the words below correctly in their spelling journals. Can they notice that certain sounds appear in other words using the same spellings?

1.	admiration	6.	ascend	11.	chaperone
2.	admission	7.	basically	12.	chic
3.	aggression	8.	boutique	13.	civilization
4.	aloud	9.	casually	14.	cliché
5.	antiseptic	10.	chandelier	15.	cohesion

For answers see www.thetrainingspace.co.uk/answers

Lens: Understanding Plurals

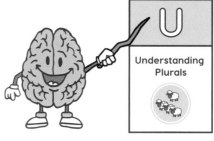

GROUPINGS

10 MINUTES

Plurals are a big area of understanding. Most singular nouns form the plural by adding –s, e.g. boat to boats, house to houses.

However, if the singular noun ends in 's', 'x', 'ch' or 'sh' you make a plural by adding –es, e.g. bus to buses and pitch to pitches. If the singular noun ends in 'y' then this is dropped and replaced with –ies, e.g. penny to pennies.

However, there are also some irregular noun plurals, e.g. woman to women, child to children, mouse to mice. To make it even harder, some plurals are the same in the singular form, e.g. sheep, fish, species, aircraft.

Learning
Words that end in consonant and 'y',   **drop and replace with –ies to pluralise.**

Words		
baby	family	money
factory	story	tray
variety	sky	body
memory	donkey	key

Question
Can you make these words plural?

Lens: Good Endings/ Suffixes

Good Endings/ Suffixes

GROUPINGS

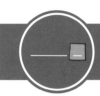

STICK!

10 MINUTES

Can you add the right **suffix** to these **verbs** to form **nouns**?

Learning
-tion and -sion are used to form nouns from verbs

Words	
inform	decide
multiply	divide
repeat	collide

Questions
Can you collect any more?
Do you have to make any changes to these words? e.g. add extra letters or remove letters.

For answers see www.thetrainingspace.co.uk/answers

Lens: Noticing Families and Roots

ACQUIRING

Build the Spell

 FLICK!

10 MINUTES

How many new words can you build using the **prefixes** and **suffixes**?
e.g. replay

Prefixes*		LEARNING You might need to drop or change or add letters when adding a suffix.	Suffixes*	
Means	**Examples**		**Examples**	**Means**
Apart	dis- dif- di-		-ful -ous -ious	Much/ Full of/ Fill
Not/ Opposite	non- un- im- in- il- ir-	soft	-ship	Position held
			-sion -tion	State of being
			-ic -ial	Having the form
With/ Together	co- com- con-	fix	-ive	Nature of
			-ment	Condition
			-ness	Quality
Cause to	em- en-	dress	-ance -ence	State
Again	re-		-ing	Action
Against	anti-	play	-ery	Place of Work
Reverse/ Remove	de-		-age	Result
Wrongly	mis-	rude	-ible -able	Ability
			-ish	Little
Before	fore-		-ly	Characteristic
Between	inter-		-y	Without

Challenge: Can you try new combinations with your own root or base words?

*This is not an exhaustive list

Lens: Order of Letters

Order of Letters

qu

IMPROVING

Spells Within Spells

 TICK!

10 MINUTES

How many words can you create from the letters provided by one word?

Remember, no names, no rude words, no brands.

1. illustration

allusion	also	alto			

Try these 4 words within words. How many words can you create by using the letters included in these words?

machinery	devotion
beautiful	flashlight

For answers see www.thetrainingspace.co.uk/answers

Lens: Verification

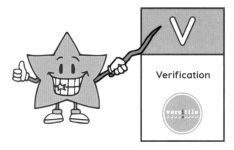

Verification

IMPROVING

Mouse Mystery

versitile

CLICK!

10 MINUTES

The cheeky mice have been nibbling at the spell book.

Can you replace the missing letters?

1.	in_ _ _ ion	11.	tr_ _ure
2.	ma_ _ine	12.	in_ _nt_on
3.	_ _correct	13.	expre_ _i_n
4.	ei_ _t	14.	bicy_ _ _
5.	char_ _ter	15.	bro_ _ure
6.	divi_ _ _ _	16.	s_ _headi_ _
7.	di_ _er_ _ _	17.	vari_us
8.	i_mature	18.	hesi_ _ _ion
9.	anti_ue	19.	disa_ _oin_
10.	ad_ _ _ture	20.	in_ _rmation

Lens: **Prefixes**

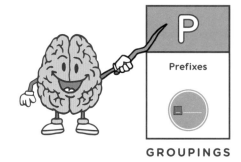

Prefixes

GROUPINGS

 # Investigation 9

30 MINUTES

Hypothesis:

un- and **dis-** can be used with root words
to create antonyms.

Believe it or not?

How many can pupils generate by themselves?

un- and **dis-**

Do you think the hypothesis is correct?

True 👍	False 👎	Sometimes 🤚

Pupil Page

Example Word List:

Teacher introduces some words to develop thinking. Use your professional judgement to introduce words during this investigation to push the learning on.

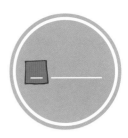

un-	dis-
unkind	distrust

kind	please	usual	happy
trust	obey	seen	tidy
popular	agree	order	lucky
connect	qualify	honest	pleasure
like	selfish	certain	approve

Key Learning:

☑ Just add un- and dis- to create an opposing meaning.

☑ Just add prefix which accounts for double 'n' unnecessary.

Teacher Support

P92

Lens: Rely on Phonics

R

Rely on Phonics

IMPROVING

Go Grapheme Grafters!

Spelling Practice

🕐 20 MINUTES

Please note all the words outlined for Year 3 cover focus areas in the National Curriculum.

Focus on these fifteen words on a cycle of two weeks, but go beyond seeing how they cope with the spelling, and target how to remember the tricky parts. This is not to be used as a spelling test. Teach spelling as a problem solving process; a mission to remember spelling for life. In the first instance, show pupils how to combine relying on phonics, then how to use visual and aural emphasis for the difficult bits. Personal problem spellings are identified and targeted through their 'Focus Five'. Encourage your pupils to be 'brave spellers' and to look closely at their mistakes so they can improve, with practice, and commit correct spellings to their long-term memory.

Learning
Look at the sound associations in the word commission. If a pupil can spell 'commission', then they know that <si> can spell the sound /ʃ/ in the following words: permission, expression, depression, admission, discussion.

Spell It Out!
Encourage your pupils to spell the words below correctly in their spelling journals. Can they notice that certain sounds appear in other words using the same spellings?

1.	commission	6.	creature	11.	discussion
2.	compassion	7.	curious	12.	dramatically
3.	comprehension	8.	cycle	13.	enclosure
4.	confession	9.	descend	14.	enormous
5.	country	10.	disagree	15.	ensure

For answers see www.thetrainingspace.co.uk/answers

Lens: Prefixes

Prefixes

GROUPINGS

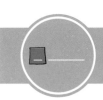

QUICK!

10 MINUTES

Understanding **prefixes** will mean pupils will learn the general principles for applying them. Certain **prefixes** hold meaning and they can support their spelling and vocabulary extension.

Learning
sub- is a prefix that can be added to words. 'sub' means under, beneath or below.
Question
How many of the following words can you add sub- to?
Words

heading	merge
marine	way
city	act
link	text
sided	national
divide	scribe

Lens: Recognising Punctuation

Recognising
Punctuation

GROUPINGS

STICK!

10 MINUTES

Words sound the same but have different meanings. Knowing the types of punctuation that are used within words, e.g. **apostrophes** and **hyphens**. Understanding the function of these punctuation marks ensures proper usage. These two are different.

Learning
It's = contracted form of it is Its = belonging to it

Words

1. "Whose bag is this?" said Mrs Franks, "_ _ _ mine!" said Ben.

2. _ _ _ a rainy day today.

3. The elephant raised _ _ _ trunk.

4. The dog opened _ _ _ mouth and barked.

Question

Can you show which is the correct one to include?
It's or Its
Can you invent other sentences to test?

Lens: Inspecting a Dictionary

Inspecting a Dictionary

IMPROVING

 ## Wonky Wand!

 FLICK!

10 MINUTES

The wizard rebuilt the dictionary with the wonky, shaky wand.
Sometimes he has got the spelling **right** and sometimes he has got it **wrong**!

You Decide!

Definition		Correct Spelling?		Make it Right
Facts and information acquired through education	knowledge		✓	
A building containing collections of books	liberary	✗		library
Drugs to prevent and treat diseases	medicine			
Badly behaved	naughty			
Well liked person or group	popurlar			
A declaration that something will or won't happen	promiss			
A sentence expressed to elicit information	question			
To rule as a monarch	reign			
An unexpected event	surprise			
The heaviness of a person/object	wait			

Can you provide the correct spelling?
Challenge: Can you put all of the words into alphabetical order?

Lens: Navigating a Thesaurus

Opposite Overturn

The Fairy Spellmother is taking all the **negative words** from the Jumping Jinx and turning them into **positive words**. Help her change the words.

e.g. rude	polite
unkind	
stupid	
nervous	
cold	
disloyal	
irresponsible	
uncaring	
tactless	
inflexible	

For answers see www.thetrainingspace.co.uk/answers

Lens: Guesses

Guesses

IMPROVING

Curses

CLICK!

10 MINUTES

Prefix

The prefix **dis-** hasn't always been put in front of the right word.
Can you check these words and if wrong, can you make the correct suggestion?

Words	Correct	Incorrect	Make it right
disrespectful	✓		
disexcusable		✗	inexcusable
disactive			
dissufferable			
dissane			
dishonest			
discorrect			
distasteful			
disgrace			
disdecent			
dishonourable			
disgusting			
disfected			
disappointing			
disadequate			
distrustful			
disagreeable			
dissidious			
diseffective			

Lens: Prefixes

Prefixes

GROUPINGS

 Investigation 10

30 MINUTES

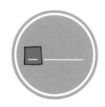

Hypothesis:

The meaning of **re-** means **'again'** and this can be useful in explaining all words that use the prefix **re-** attached to a whole word.

Believe it or not?

How many can pupils generate by themselves?

re-

Do you think the hypothesis is correct?

True 👍	False 👎	Sometimes 👋

Pupil Page

Example Word List:

Teacher introduces some words to develop thinking. Use your professional judgement to introduce words during this investigation to push the learning on.

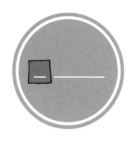

	Definition
rebound	To bounce back (a ball in a sporting context)
rebuild	
recycle	
refill	
reform	
retreat	
recede	
return	
replace	
revisit	
replay	
reunite	
repay	

Key Learning

☑ The word prefix has the prefix **pre-** and can help you define it.

☑ **re-** means **'again'**.

☑ Words that include this prefix mean **rewind**, **redo** and **repeat**.

Teacher Support

Lens: Rely on Phonics

Rely on
Phonics

IMPROVING

Go Grapheme Grafters!

Spelling Practice

20 MINUTES

Please note all the words outlined for Year 3 cover focus areas in the National Curriculum.

Focus on these fifteen words on a cycle of two weeks, but go beyond seeing how they cope with the spelling, and target how to remember the tricky parts. This is not to be used as a spelling test. Teach spelling as a problem solving process; a mission to remember spelling for life. In the first instance, show pupils how to combine relying on phonics, then how to use visual and aural emphasis for the difficult bits. Personal problem spellings are identified and targeted through their 'Focus Five'. Encourage your pupils to be 'brave spellers' and to look closely at their mistakes so they can improve, with practice, and commit correct spellings to their long-term memory.

Learning
Look at the sound associations in the word expansion. If a pupil can spell 'expansion', then they know that <si> can spell the sound /ʃ/ in the following words: man_si_on, exten_si_on, comprehen_si_on, ten_si_on, pen_si_on.

Spell It Out!
Encourage your pupils to spell the words below correctly in their spelling journals. Can they notice that certain sounds appear in other words using the same spellings?

1.	expansion	6.	February	11.	furniture
2.	experiment	7.	frantically	12.	gardener
3.	extreme	8.	freight	13.	gardening
4.	famous	9.	fruit	14.	groan
5.	favourite	10.	furious	15.	group

For answers see www.thetrainingspace.co.uk/answers

Lens: Prefixes

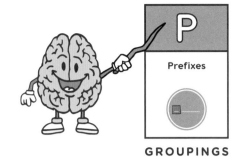

Prefixes

GROUPINGS

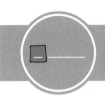

QUICK!

10 MINUTES

Understanding **prefixes** will mean pupils will learn general principles for applying them. Certain **prefixes** hold meaning and they can support their spelling and vocabulary extension.

Which words can you add the prefix in-?

Learning
in- means not and into. Before a root word starting with 'l' in- becomes il-. Before a root word starting with 'm' or 'p' in- becomes im-

Words		
in		
perfect	legible	possible
legal	moral	active
mature	patient	correct

Question
Can you add prefix in- or il- or im-?

Lens: Good Endings/ Suffixes

GROUPINGS

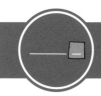

STICK!

🕐 10 MINUTES

Can you turn these **present tense** verbs into the **past tense**?

Learning
These are regular verbs.

Words	
present tense	**past tense**
help	helped
turn	
sort	
wash	
rock	
roll	
call	
laugh	

Question
Can you change these words into the past tense? Can you add more?

Lens: Analogies

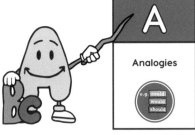

Analogies

ACQUIRING

Charm Chaser

FLICK!

10 MINUTES

Can you collect words with the letter string **'ick'**?
For every three words you collect you win a charm!

e.g. carsick or rickets

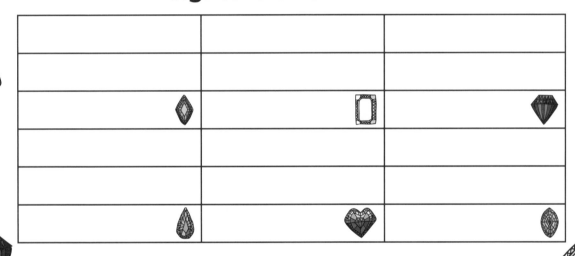

Can you collect words with the letter string **'ale'**?

e.g. telltale or folktale

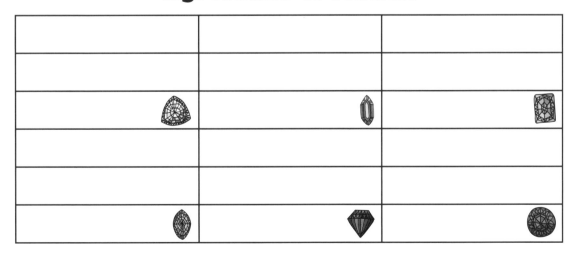

Why not try to find as many words as you can
with these letter strings – **'ap'**, **'aw'**, **'ay'**, **'eat'**?

Lens: Check Etymology

Etymology Ladders

TICK!

10 MINUTES

Pattern Climber

All of these words have a component that means the same thing.
Can you identify the word and the meaning of the prefix?

Hint: All definitions mention 'self' in the clue.

Clue	Answer beginning with self-
1. Car that moves by it 'self'	
2. A setting on a plane where the plane flies by it 'self'	
3. Robot which moves by it 'self'	
4. Life history written by the person about themselves	
5. Of rule by the 'self'	
6. A camera function where it focuses it 'self'	
7. Signature written by a person (themselves)	
8. Pertaining to a process which moves by it 'self'	

For answers see www.thetrainingspace.co.uk/answers

Lens: Quiz Yourself

Quiz
Yourself

ACQUIRING

Spelling Study Time

CLICK!

10 MINUTES

Design a bank of 10 words that pupils know they struggle to spell
(look at independent writing).

1. Look closely at the word. Is there a part that reminds them of another word, e.g. guitar like guess or guest?

2. Could over pronunciation help? Many words that are tricky to spell are the unstressed vowel sounds. Over pronouncing February helps you remember the letter 'r', e.g. Feb/ru/ary e.g. bus/i/ness.

3. Can you split the word into prefix, root word, suffix, e.g. uncleanliness?

4. Identify tricky bits and try to zoom into these and think of ditties or silly things to commit to memory, e.g. the word relevant – don't make the small ant-like mistake of adding ent instead of ant, the word library – there's a bra in the library.

5. Add a drawing or quick visual to help you. A '2' drawn in-between the two 'ls' in marvel²lous reminds you to add two 'ls'.

My word	My spell check	Omitted letters	Extra letters	Both	Other	Advice for myself
there	their				wrong homophone	i belongs to them
ataked	attacked			x		two t's attack ck
discusting	disgusting				x	gust of wind is disgusting
jumpt	jumped				forgot past tense ending	regular verb

Share ideas and strategies with your class.

For answers see www.thetrainingspace.co.uk/answers

Lens: Irregular/ Exception Words

Irregular/ Exception Words

GROUPINGS

Investigation 11

30 MINUTES

words

Hypothesis:

An irregular verb is a word that changes from present to past, e.g.		
past	past progressive	present
run	running	ran
have	having	had

Believe it or not?

How many can pupils generate by themselves?

Do you think the hypothesis is correct?

True 👍	False 👎	Sometimes 〰️

Pupil Page

Example Word List:

Teacher introduces some words to develop thinking. Use your professional judgement to introduce words during this investigation to push the learning on.

Regular	Irregular
agree	take
add	have
arrive	go
cross	do
enjoy	make
	dress

Key Learning

☑ A regular verb follows the normal pattern of inflection, e.g the general rule is regular verbs form the past tense by adding -ed.

☑ An irregular verb changers when used in the past tense, e.g 'write' changes to 'wrote' therefore irregular.

Lens: Rely on Phonics

Rely on Phonics

IMPROVING

Go Grapheme Grafters!

Spelling Practice

20 MINUTES

Please note all the words outlined for Year 3 cover focus areas in the National Curriculum.

Focus on these fifteen words on a cycle of two weeks, but go beyond seeing how they cope with the spelling, and target how to remember the tricky parts. This is not to be used as a spelling test. Teach spelling as a problem solving process; a mission to remember spelling for life. In the first instance, show pupils how to combine relying on phonics, then how to use visual and aural emphasis for the difficult bits. Personal problem spellings are identified and targeted through their 'Focus Five'. Encourage your pupils to be 'brave spellers' and to look closely at their mistakes so they can improve, with practice, and commit correct spellings to their long-term memory.

Learning
Look at the sound associations in the word grown. If a pupil can spell 'grown', then they know that <ow> can spell the sound /əʊ/ in the following words: blown, known, thrown, window, shallow.

Spell It Out!
Encourage your pupils to spell the words below correctly in their spelling journals. Can they notice that certain sounds appear in other words using the same spellings?

1.	grown	6.	heart	11.	imagine
2.	guide	7.	heel	12.	immortal
3.	heal	8.	here	13.	important
4.	hear	9.	history	14.	incorrect
5.	heard	10.	illusion	15.	interest

For answers see www.thetrainingspace.co.uk/answers

Lens: Irregular/ Exception Words

GROUPINGS

QUICK!

10 MINUTES

Certain words do not follow patterns and these could be for phonetic reasons or systems for pluralising. There are irregular words that need to be learnt.

Learning
/s/ sound spelt as 'c' before 'e', 'i', and 'y'. This can cause spelling problems.

Words	
bicycle	centre
century	certain
circle	decision
decide	exercise
experience	medicine
notice	

Question
Can you learn these words perfectly?

For answers see www.thetrainingspace.co.uk/answers

Lens: Understanding Plurals

Understanding
Plurals

GROUPINGS

STICK!

10 MINUTES

Plurals are a big area of understanding. Most singular nouns form the plural by adding –s, e.g. boat to boats, house to houses.

However, if the singular noun ends in 's', 'x', 'ch' or 'sh' you make a plural by adding -es, e.g. bus to buses and pitch to pitches. If the singular noun ends in 'y' then this is dropped and replaced with –ies, e.g. penny to pennies.

However, there are also some irregular noun plurals, e.g. woman to women, child to children, mouse to mice. To make it even harder, some plurals are the same in the singular form, e.g. sheep, fish, species, aircraft.

Learning
If words end in 'ch', 'zz', 'sh', 's', or 'x', an -es is required to pluralise.

Words		
stop	bunch	dish
boat	fizz	fox
goal	match	thank
buzz	park	mend
cross	bark	circus
fuss	crash	melt

Question
Do you need to add -s or -es to make plural?

For answers see www.thetrainingspace.co.uk/answers

Lens: Understanding Patterns

Understanding Patterns

ACQUIRING

Perfect Concoction

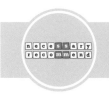

FLICK!

10 MINUTES

How many new words can you create using different combinations of prefixes and suffixes?

Prefixes		in-	il-	super-	sub-
Suffixes		-ment	-ness	-ful	-less	-ly

Prefix +	Root word	+ Suffix	New Word
in-	sane	-ly	insane, sanely
	vent		
	side		
	sight		
	luminate		
	legal		
	logical		
	hero		
	size		
	merge		
	group		
	heart		
	point		
	cheer		

How many words can you make out of these prefixes, root words and suffixes?

You might just choose a prefix and root word, e.g. unhappy

You might just choose a root word and a suffix, e.g. happiest

You might be able to use both a prefix and suffix with a root word, e.g. unhappiest

For answers see www.thetrainingspace.co.uk/answers

Lens: I/Me Personal Spelling

ACQUIRING

My Focus Five

 **TICK!**

Personal Spells I Need to Target!

10 MINUTES

This information might come from Go Grapheme Grafters or from analysis of independent writing. Pupils or teachers can decide the five to target.

My Focus Five	Say it! Secure it! Sort it!	Pupil evidence used correctly in their writing			Teacher signs off
Example: disgusting	discusting puts a 'c' instead of 'g' disgusting				
1					
2					
3					
4					
5					
Name:					
Week Beginning:					

For answers see www.thetrainingspace.co.uk/answers

Lens: Recognising Parts

ACQUIRING

Fix It!

CLICK!

10 MINUTES

Prefix or Suffix or Both

Can you build new words by adding on a prefix or suffix or both?

Prefix pre-	Root Word	Suffix 'ing'	Prefix	Suffix	Both
pre-	script	-ion	prescript	scription	prescription
	object				
	destruct				
	alliterate				
	mission				
	form				
	cent				
	impress				
	pollute				

Lens: Irregular/ Exception Words

 Investigation 12

30 MINUTES

Hypothesis:

An irregular verb is a word that changes from present to past.

Believe it or not?

Which group would you place each word in?
What is the tricky part? Why?

Do you think the hypothesis is correct?

True 👍	False 👎	Sometimes 🖐

Pupil Page

Example Word List:

Teacher introduces some words to develop thinking. Use your professional judgement to introduce words during this investigation to push the learning on.

short vowel verbs	-ed	-ing
drags		
drops		
grabs		
swims		
hugs		
stops		
shops		
plans		
flops		
claps		
knits		
hops		

Key Learning

☑ If the word has a short vowel sound, then you must add a double letter before -ed and -ing.

☑ The past and progressive past tense of these words will have a double letter.

Lens: Rely on Phonics

Rely on
Phonics

IMPROVING

Go Grapheme Grafters!

Spelling Practice

20 MINUTES

Please note all the words outlined for Year 3 cover focus areas in the National Curriculum.

Focus on these fifteen words on a cycle of two weeks, but go beyond seeing how they cope with the spelling, and target how to remember the tricky parts. This is not to be used as a spelling test. Teach spelling as a problem solving process; a mission to remember spelling for life. In the first instance, show pupils how to combine relying on phonics, then how to use visual and aural emphasis for the difficult bits. Personal problem spellings are identified and targeted through their 'Focus Five'. Encourage your pupils to be 'brave spellers' and to look closely at their mistakes so they can improve, with practice, and commit correct spellings to their long-term memory.

Learning
Look at the sound associations in the word irrelevant. If a pupil can spell 'irrelevant', then they know that <i> can spell the sound /ɪ/ in the following words: irregular, irresponsible, irrational, irresistible, irreversible.

Spell It Out!
Encourage your pupils to spell the words below correctly in their spelling journals. Can they notice that certain sounds appear in other words using the same spellings?

1.	irrelevant	6.	library	11.	musician
2.	jealous	7.	limited	12.	obey
3.	learn	8.	limiting	13.	obvious
4.	leisure	9.	mechanic	14.	passion
5.	length	10.	mislead	15.	piece

For answers see www.thetrainingspace.co.uk/answers

Lens: Irregular/ Exception Words

Irregular/ Exception Words

GROUPINGS

QUICK!

10 MINUTES

Certain words do not follow patterns and these could be for phonetic reasons or systems for pluralising. There are irregular words that need to be learnt.

Learning
Unstressed vowels **can cause spelling problems. These words have** unstressed vowels.

Words		
different	February	library
family	separate	centre
favourite	interest	ordinary
secretary	poisons	original

Question
Can you identify the part that causes spelling problems?

Lens: Recognising Punctuation

R

Recognising
Punctuation

GROUPINGS

STICK!

10 MINUTES

Knowing the types of punctuation that are used within words, e.g.
apostrophes. Understanding the function of these punctuation marks
ensures proper usage.

Learning
Apostrophes **are used to show omitted letters when two words are** contracted **together.**

Words	
she'll	she's
couldn't	I've
it'll	they'll
they're	didn't
can't	he's
I'm	I'd

Question
Can you identify the positive contractions **in this list?**

For answers see www.thetrainingspace.co.uk/answers

Lens: Illustrative

Illustrative

ACQUIRING

Themed Words

FLICK!

10 MINUTES

The Garden

1.

2.

3.

4.

5.

6.

10.

8.

9.

7.

Can you label this picture with accurately spelt words?
Can you draw your own picture and label it?

Lens: Noticing Families and Roots

Noticing Families and Roots

ACQUIRING

Web of Words

TICK!

10 MINUTES

Can you provide the word that matches the **definition**?

1. Made by hand	m _ _ m a _ _
2. Lead by example	_ _ n _ g e
3. Taking care of the hands	_ a n i _ _ _ _
4. Animal fertiliser (in the old days spread 'by hand')	_ _ n u r _
5. Social politeness	_ _ n n _ _ s
6. To operate by hand	_ a _ u _ l

Challenge

What is the root word?
Can you add any more words with this root?

For answers see www.thetrainingspace.co.uk/answers

Lens: Go! Speed! Write!

Go! Speed! Write!

ACQUIRING

Exploding Potions

 **CLICK!**

10 MINUTES

Test each other across these **three categories**.

1 min Challenge	1 min Challenge	1 min Challenge
Numbers 41 - 60	Colours of the rainbow	Garden themed words
Can you spell all 20?	How many colours did you spell correctly?	How many words did you think of?

Lens: New Meaning/ Homophone

New Meaning/ Homophone

GROUPINGS

Investigation 13

30 MINUTES

Hypothesis:

All **compound words** include silent letters

Believe it or not?

Sort words into two groups

Long vowel phonemes		Silent letters

Do you think the hypothesis is correct?

Pupil Page

True 👍	False 👎	Sometimes 👐

Example Word List:

Teacher introduces some words to develop thinking. Use your professional judgement to introduce words during this investigation to push the learning on.

horseshoe	playground	swordfish
handwrite	shipwreck	bluebell
football	weekend	anywhere
popcorn	cupboard	kneepad
wristband	deadline	penknife
churchyard	knighthood	thumbnail
blackbird	lighthouse	gunpowder
greenhouse	goalkeeper	drawbridge
earthworm	paintbrush	knucklebone
upstairs	daylight	breakfast

Key Learning

☑ A **compound word** is made up from two words joined together with no space.

☑ Break a compound word into two parts as this will make it easier to spell.

☑ Silent letters can occur in any type of word. The letter **'k'** and **'g'** can be silent cubits.

Lens: Rely on Phonics

Go Grapheme Grafters!

Spelling Practice

20 MINUTES

Please note all the words outlined for Year 3 cover focus areas in the National Curriculum.

Focus on these fifteen words on a cycle of two weeks, but go beyond seeing how they cope with the spelling, and target how to remember the tricky parts. This is not to be used as a spelling test. Teach spelling as a problem solving process; a mission to remember spelling for life. In the first instance, show pupils how to combine relying on phonics, then how to use visual and aural emphasis for the difficult bits. Personal problem spellings are identified and targeted through their 'Focus Five'. Encourage your pupils to be 'brave spellers' and to look closely at their mistakes so they can improve, with practice, and commit correct spellings to their long-term memory.

Learning
Look at the sound associations in the word plague. If a pupil can spell 'plague', then they know that <gue> can spell the sound /g/ in the following words: vague, rogue, vogue, league, morgue.

Spell It Out!
Encourage your pupils to spell the words below correctly in their spelling journals. Can they notice that certain sounds appear in other words using the same spellings?

1.	plague	6.	unusual	11.	water
2.	tinsel	7.	usual	12.	we'll
3.	told	8.	walk	13.	worm
4.	towards	9.	wander	14.	woman's book
5.	tropical	10.	warp	15.	worth

For answers see www.thetrainingspace.co.uk/answers

Lens: New Meaning/ Homophone

N

New Meaning/ Homophone

GROUPINGS

Compound Words

QUICK!

10 MINUTES

Compound words are two words in their own right that join and make a new word. There is often an associated meaning.

Learning
A **compound word** is a combination of two words that function as a single word and a single unit of meaning.

Words			
cowboy	roundabout	however	girlfriend
nowadays	birthday	herself	boyfriend
cornflakes	thirteen	carpark	farmhouse
greenhouse	halftime	doorstep	moreover
yourself	outcome	fourteen	shoreline

Question
Can you sort these compound words into those with a long vowel sound? Can you add an example, e.g. fourteen? /aʊ/ /ɔɪ/ /ɜː/ /ʊə/ /ɑː/?

Lens: Recognising Punctuation

R

Recognising Punctuation

GROUPINGS

STICK!

10 MINUTES

A **proper noun** is a specific name for a particular **person**, **place** or **thing**. Proper nouns always begin with a **capital letter**, regardless of where they are in a sentence.

Learning
All proper nouns **require a capital letter regardless of where they fall in the sentence.**

Words	
John	January
Mary	Sunday
England	Spiderman
London	Pepsi
McDonalds	Porsche

Question
Can you add any more proper nouns**?**   **Can you sort them into** groups**?**

For answers see www.thetrainingspace.co.uk/answers

Lens: Interrogate and Check

Spot the Spells

FLICK!

10 MINUTES

Can you find the **9 spelling errors** in this piece of work and edit it to the correct **spellings**?

Dear Dairy,
This morning, my brother had an acident on his bicycle. The road was really busi. A car hit his back whel. Thankfully, he wasn't badly hert. He had a cut on his knree and kneeded medisine and promuses not to ride for a while.

(9 Errors)

1. ☐   4. ☐   7. ☐

2. ☐   5. ☐   8. ☐

3. ☐   6. ☐   9. ☐

Lens: Order of Letters

Order of
Letters

qu

IMPROVING

Spells Within Spells

qu   **TICK!**   10 MINUTES

How many words can you create from the **letters** provided by one word?

Remember, no names, no rude words, no brands.

unauthorised

oars	snout	trio	art		

Try these 4 words within words. How many
words can you create by using the letters
included in these words?

mother	snowstorm
dinosaur	pretending

For answers see www.thetrainingspace.co.uk/answers

Lens: Verification

Verification

IMPROVING

Good Spells Vs Bad Spells

CLICK!

10 MINUTES

Can you sort this list into good spellings and bad spellings?
Can you identify the bad spellings and correct them?

Learning				
beginner ✓	forgoton ✗	disappoint	inactive	country
prefer	illegal	limition	imposible	interact
limited	reappear	mystery	irrelevant	finaly
touch	subdivide	truble	sensation	disobey

Good Spells	Bad Spells
beginner	forgoton ➡ forgotten

Lens: New Meaning/ Homophone

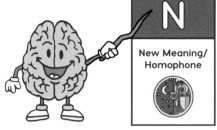

GROUPINGS

Investigation 14

30 MINUTES

Hypothesis:

If you test your class mates on the following **20 words**.
They will all get the same words wrong.

Believe it or not?

Can you predict the mistakes your classmates will make?

Do you think the hypothesis is correct?

True 👍	False 👎	Sometimes 🖐

Pupil Page

Example Word List:

Teacher introduces some words to develop thinking. Use your professional judgement to introduce words during this investigation to push the learning on.

20 Spellings	How many got correct?	What is tricky part of this word?
across		
although		
beautiful		
believe		
caught		
children		
clothes		
definitely		
different		
embarrass		
excellent		
favourite		
interesting		
mountain		
people		
question		

Key Learning

☑ Many words in English cause problems.

☑ Try and identify the part that was tricky to sort for the next time.

Lens: Rely on Phonics

Rely on
Phonics

IMPROVING

Go Grapheme Grafters!

Spelling Practice

20 MINUTES

Please note all the words outlined for Year 3 cover focus areas in the National Curriculum.

Focus on these fifteen words on a cycle of two weeks, but go beyond seeing how they cope with the spelling, and target how to remember the tricky parts. This is not to be used as a spelling test. Teach spelling as a problem solving process; a mission to remember spelling for life. In the first instance, show pupils how to combine relying on phonics, then how to use visual and aural emphasis for the difficult bits. Personal problem spellings are identified and targeted through their 'Focus Five'. Encourage your pupils to be 'brave spellers' and to look closely at their mistakes so they can improve, with practice, and commit correct spellings to their long-term memory.

Learning
Look at the sound associations in the word unique. If a pupil can spell 'unique', then they know that <que> can spell the sound /k/ in the following words: antique, plaque, mosque, cheque, technique.

Spell It Out!
Encourage your pupils to spell the words below correctly in their spelling journals. Can they notice that certain sounds appear in other words using the same spellings?

1.	unique	6.	able	11.	girl's pen
2.	wreck	7.	after	12.	break
3.	wrinkle	8.	alley	13.	busy
4.	writer	9.	bath	14.	caption
5.	you're	10.	beautiful	15.	cartwheel

For answers see www.thetrainingspace.co.uk/answers

Lens: New Meaning/ Homophone

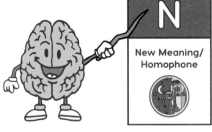

GROUPINGS

Homophones

QUICK!

10 MINUTES

Homophones are words that have the same pronunciation but different spelling and meaning. Near homophones cause many spelling confusions.

Learning
Homophones are words that sound the same but are spelt differently with a different meaning.

Words			
brake	**break**	grate	
heel		main	
missed		plain	
peace		groan	
mail		meat	
medal		here	

Question
Can you provide definitions for these words?

Lens: Organising Sounds

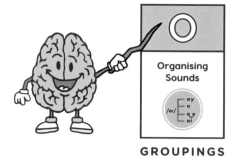

STICK!

10 MINUTES

Listening carefully to phonemes and syllables. Knowing there are good phonic and letter string guesses for common sounds. Learning how to make the most plausible choices.

Learning
'a' is the most common spelling for /ɒ/ ('what'). It is a common sound after 'w' and 'qu' and 'sq' and is represented with the letter 'a'.

Words	
want	watch
wander	wand
wasp	was
wallet	warrant
wad	wash

Question
How many words can you think of where 'a' is the letter that follows 'w'? Can you hear the sound that 'a' makes?

For answers see www.thetrainingspace.co.uk/answers

Lens: Inspecting a Dictionary

Dictionary Disaster

FLICK!

10 MINUTES

What a disaster! These words keep changing position in the dictionary.
Help the word wizard put them in **alphabetical order**.

Jumbled Order	Dictionary Order 1
1. antique	1.
2. antelope	2.
3. answer	3.
4. another	4.
5. anxious	5.

Jumbled Order	Dictionary Order 2
1. certain	1.
2. chain	2.
3. celebrate	3.
4. caught	4.
5. cemetery	5.

Lens: Navigating a Thesaurus

IMPROVING

Synonym Spectacular

TICK!

10 MINUTES

Can you add in the missing letters for the words
in the same **synonym family**?

s _ _ _ _ _ _ c u _ _ r ➤ s p e c t a c u l a r	
Amazing	1. _ _ _ s o m e
	2. i n c _ _ _ _ _ _ _
	3. f a s _ _ _ _ _ _ n g
	4. m _ _ _ _ l l _ _ _

5. s t u _ _ n _ _
6. a _ t o n _ _ _ i n g
7. w _ _ _ _ _ f u l
8. s u _ _ _ _ _ i n g
9. u n _ _ _ _ _ _ a b l e

a p p _ _ _ _ i n g ➤ a p p e t i s i n g	
Delicious	1. d e _ _ _ _ a b l e
	2. d e _ _ _ _ _ f u l
	3. l _ _ _ i o u s
	4. r _ _ h

5. s _ _ _ _ _ y
6. t _ _ _ y
7. s _ e _ _
8. t _ _ _ t i n g
9. y _ _ _ y

Can you use a **thesaurus** to add more?

For answers see www.thetrainingspace.co.uk/answers

Lens: Guesses

Guesses

IMPROVING

Spells & Smells & Potions & Notions!

CLICK!

10 MINUTES

Take turns in pairs. One of your pair will have the answers ready, whilst the other one has to work out the hidden word.

Can you correctly find the word within **ten guesses**? Each wrong letter guess adds a spoonful of liquid.

Make sure the potion doesn't **explode**.

Definition	Letters	Amount of guesses
When you can't remember something.	_ _ _ g _ t _ _ _	1 2 3 4 5 6 7 8 9 **10**
When you like something more than something else.	_ r _ f _ _	1 2 3 4 5 6 7 8 9 **10**
When you tidy and plant outside.	_ a _ d _ _ _ _ _	1 2 3 4 5 6 7 8 9 **10**
When you have a problem.	t _ _ _ b _ _	1 2 3 4 5 6 7 8 9 **10**
When you fail to live up to expectations.	d _ _ _ p p _ _ _ _	1 2 3 4 5 6 7 8 9 **10**
When you are naughty.	_ _ _ b _ h _ v _	1 2 3 4 5 6 7 8 9 **10**

Lens: Group/Year Specific

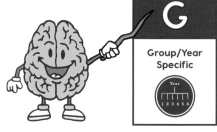

Group/Year
Specific

GROUPINGS

Investigation 15

30 MINUTES

Hypothesis:

From the following selection **'ear'**, **'ight'**, **'on'**, **'au'**, **'ice'**...
'an' is the most common letter string used in the largest
majority in English words

Believe it or not?

How many can pupils generate by themselves?

Do you think the hypothesis is correct?

Pupil Page

True 👍	False 👎	Sometimes 〰️

Example Word List:

Teacher introduces some words to develop thinking. Use your professional judgement to introduce words during this investigation to push the learning on.

	ear	ight	on	au	ice
light		✕			
haunt					
weight					
bear					
hearth					
twice					
height					
sauce					
route					
freight					
gear					

Key Learning

☑ The same letter string can be used to represent different **phonemes**.

☑ Same letter strings create different **pronunciations** but some are more common than others, e.g. **weight**, **eight**, **freight** (less common).

Lens: Rely on Phonics

Rely on Phonics

IMPROVING

Go Grapheme Grafters!

 Spelling Practice

20 MINUTES

Please note all the words outlined for Year 3 cover focus areas in the National Curriculum.

Focus on these fifteen words on a cycle of two weeks, but go beyond seeing how they cope with the spelling, and target how to remember the tricky parts. This is not to be used as a spelling test. Teach spelling as a problem solving process; a mission to remember spelling for life. In the first instance, show pupils how to combine relying on phonics, then how to use visual and aural emphasis for the difficult bits. Personal problem spellings are identified and targeted through their 'Focus Five'. Encourage your pupils to be 'brave spellers' and to look closely at their mistakes so they can improve, with practice, and commit correct spellings to their long-term memory.

Learning
Look at the sound associations in the word comprehension. If a pupil can spell 'comprehension', then they know that \<c\> can spell the sound /k/ in the following words: complete, concrete, concussion, container, contact.

Spell It Out!
Encourage your pupils to spell the words below correctly in their spelling journals. Can they notice that certain sounds appear in other words using the same spellings?

1.	comprehension	6.	counsel	11.	cycle
2.	centre	7.	cover	12.	daffodil
3.	circular	8.	cried	13.	definition
4.	class	9.	cruel	14.	dimple
5.	clothes	10.	crying	15.	eagle

For answers see www.thetrainingspace.co.uk/answers

Lens: Group/Year Specific

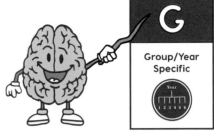

Group/Year
Specific

GROUPINGS

QUICK!

10 MINUTES

There are certain aspects of spelling that are relevant to different year groups.

Learning
These words should be learnt as needed. The /ɪ/ sounds spelt 'y' elsewhere than at the end of words.

Words	
myth	mith
gym	gim
Egipt	Egypt
pyramid	piramid
mistery	mystery

Question
Can you choose the correct spelling of these words?

Lens: Organising Sounds

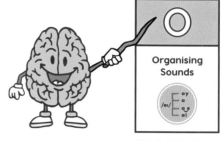

STICK!

10 MINUTES

Listening carefully to the phoneme and syllables. Knowing there are good phonic and letter string guesses for common sounds. Learning how to make the most plausible choices.

Learning
Knowing that the same sound can be represented in different ways.

Words		
still	cell	sky
pencil	race	city
face	dice	dance
fancy	acid	decent
ice	cell	civil

Question
Why is the letter 's' or 'c' making the /s/ sound?

For answers see www.thetrainingspace.co.uk/answers

Lens: Analogies

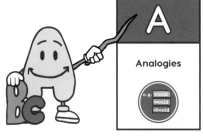

Analogies

e.g. could
would
should

ACQUIRING

Conjure a Word Storm

e.g. could
would
should

FLICK!

10 MINUTES

Using the letters below, start with one word and change one letter or diagraph (two letters) to make a new word. See if you can find a word for each box to complete the circle.

Use the following letters and sounds

s, r, b, o, i, u, a, ng, ck

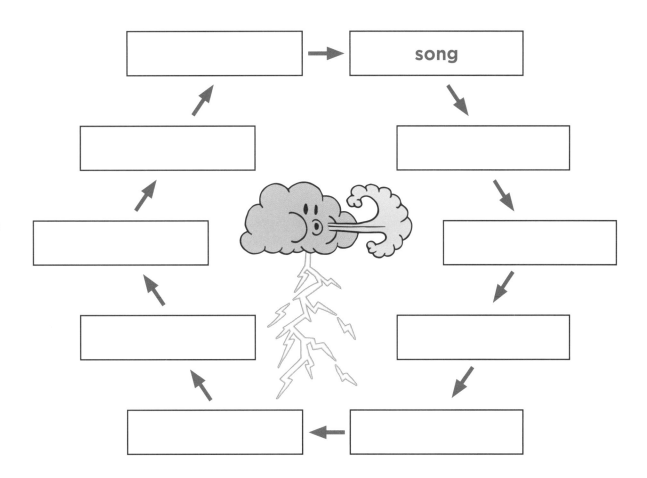

| | → | song |

You can only use a word once

Lens: Quiz Yourself

Quiz
Yourself

ACQUIRING

Spelling Study Time

TICK!

10 MINUTES

Design a bank of 10 words that pupils know they struggle to spell
(look at independent writing).

1. Look closely at the word. Is there a part that reminds them of another word, e.g. guitar like guess or guest?

2. Could over pronunciation help? Many words that are tricky to spell are the unstressed vowel sounds. Over pronouncing February helps you remember the letter 'r', e.g. Feb/ru/ary e.g. bus/i/ness.

3. Can you split the word into prefix, root word, suffix, e.g. uncleanliness?

4. Identify tricky bits and try to zoom into these and think of ditties or silly things to commit to memory, e.g. the word relevant – don't make the small ant-like mistake of adding ent instead of ant, the word library – there's a bra in the library.

5. Add a drawing or quick visual to help you. A '2' drawn in-between the two 'ls' in marvel²lous reminds you to add two 'ls'.

My word	My spell check	Omitted letter/s	Extra letter/s	Both	Other	Advice for myself
there	their				wrong homophone	i belongs to them
ataked	attacked			x		two t's attack ck
discusting	disgusting				x	gust of wind is disgusting
jumpt	jumped				forgot past tense ending	regular verb

Share ideas and strategies with your class.

For answers see www.thetrainingspace.co.uk/answers

Lens: Understanding Patterns

Understanding Patterns

ACQUIRING

Spell Maker

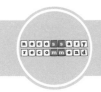 **CLICK!**

10 MINUTES

These words have become disordered when the spell went wrong.
Please rebuild correctly.

Jumbled Order	Correct order
e.g. trust ing dis	distrusting
cover re ing	
ing re paint	
view re ing	
able roll un	
un able comfort	
fold re able	
ing re open	
re ed load	
connect dis ing	

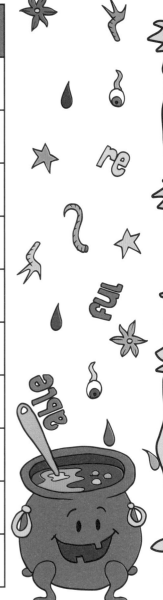

Lens: Group/Year Specific

Group/Year Specific

GROUPINGS

Investigation 16

30 MINUTES

Hypothesis:

The most common word that can be found within most other words is **'on'**.

Believe it or not?

How many can pupils generate by themselves?

Do you think the hypothesis is correct?

Pupil Page

True 👍	False 👎	Sometimes 🤚

Example Word List:

Teacher introduces some words to develop thinking. Use your professional judgement to introduce words during this investigation to push the learning on.

The words discovered need to have their letters appearing consecutively in original word	
incredible	pretending
something	wonderful
unbelievable	challenging
whatever	another

	Constable
Example: words within the word 'constable'	con
	on
	stable
	table
	tab
	able

Key Learning

☑ Recognising **words within words** develops visual strategies.

☑ Many spells lean on these visual clues to support spelling.

Lens: Rely on Phonics

IMPROVING

Go Grapheme Grafters!

 Spelling Practice

20 MINUTES

Please note all the words outlined for Year 3 cover focus areas in the National Curriculum.

Focus on these fifteen words on a cycle of two weeks, but go beyond seeing how they cope with the spelling, and target how to remember the tricky parts. This is not to be used as a spelling test. Teach spelling as a problem solving process; a mission to remember spelling for life. In the first instance, show pupils how to combine relying on phonics, then how to use visual and aural emphasis for the difficult bits. Personal problem spellings are identified and targeted through their 'Focus Five'. Encourage your pupils to be 'brave spellers' and to look closely at their mistakes so they can improve, with practice, and commit correct spellings to their long-term memory.

Learning
Look at the sound associations in the word disobey. If a pupil can spell 'disobey', then they know that <ey> can spell the sound /eɪ/ in the following words: grey, prey, survey, convey, they.

Spell It Out!
Encourage your pupils to spell the words below correctly in their spelling journals. Can they notice that certain sounds appear in other words using the same spellings?

1.	disobey	6.	fatter	11.	giraffe
2.	example	7.	fattest	12.	gnat
3.	fall	8.	final	13.	grass
4.	fast	9.	fulfil	14.	great
5.	father	10.	giant	15.	happily

For answers see www.thetrainingspace.co.uk/answers

Lens: Group/Year Specific

QUICK!

10 MINUTES

Understand that the same sounds aren't necessarily represented with the same graphemes.

Learning
The /v/ sound spelt 'ou'.

Words	
young	rough
enough	touch
tough	southern
double	couple
flourish	trouble
courage	nourish
country	cousin

Question
Can you hear the sound that the grapheme 'ou' makes in these words? Compare to 'aloud'?

Lens: New Meaning/ Homophone

N

New Meaning/ Homophone

GROUPINGS

Homophones

STICK!

10 MINUTES

Homophones are words that have the same pronunciation but different spelling and meaning. Near homophones cause many spelling confusions.

Learning
Homophones **are words that sound the same but are spelt differently with a different meaning.**

Words			
hair	hare	here	
sea		blew	
bare		knight	
role		ewe	
buy		new	

Question
Can you write a matching homophone for these words?
Can you define the different meanings by using different homophones in sentences?

For answers see www.thetrainingspace.co.uk/answers

Lens: I/Me Personal Spelling

ACQUIRING

My Focus Five

FLICK!

Personal Spells I Need to Target!

10 MINUTES

This information might come from Go Grapheme Grafters or from analysis of independent writing. Pupils or teachers can decide the five to target.

My Focus Five	Say it! Secure it! Sort it!	Pupil evidence used correctly in their writing			Teacher signs off
Example: disgusting	discusting puts a 'c' instead of 'g' disgusting				
1					
2					
3					
4					
5					
Name:					
Week Beginning:					

Lens: Recognising Parts

Broom Zoom!

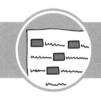

TICK!

10 MINUTES

Izzy Whizzy! Let's get busy!

Two brooms can crash together to make one word.

-ion or -ian

Do you need to add and -ion or -ian to the ending?

construct →	construction
supress →	suppression
obstruct	
product	
connect	
technic	
politic	
physic	
statistic	
arithmetic	

For answers see www.thetrainingspace.co.uk/answers

Lens: Order of Letters

Find your team

 CLICK!

10 MINUTES

Can you sort the words into the correct group when ending a '**le**'?

Learning
fiddle   sale   sensible   dale   vegetable   kettle   tadpole   nettle   dimple whale   folktale   cuddle   responsible   nozzle   upscale   cubicle mole   inhale   article   bubble   sample   stole   wobble

Word Wizard	Fairy Spell Mother	Fred the Frog
Double letter 'le'	Split digraph 'le' words	Other words that end in 'le' endings to suffixes, e.g. -ckle, -able, -cle, -dle, -ble, -ible, -ple
little	smile	grumble

Lens: **Syllables**

Investigation 17

30 MINUTES

Hypothesis:

If you can add **-ful** to a root word, you can add **-ly**.

Believe it or not?

How many can pupils generate by themselves?

Do you think the hypothesis is correct?

True 👍	False 👎	Sometimes 👋

Pupil Page

Example Word List:

Teacher introduces some words to develop thinking. Use your professional judgement to introduce words during this investigation to push the learning on.

Short vowel multisyllabic words			Long vowel multisyllabic words		
2 syllables	add -ful	add -ly	2 syllables	add -ful	add -ly
thank	thankful	thankfully	real		really
happy		happily	nice		nicely
plenty	plentiful	plentifully	moody		moodily
pity	pitiful	pitifully	smooth		smoothly
			hope	hopeful	hopefully
			peace	peaceful	peacefully
			beauty	beautiful	beautifully

Key Learning

☑ In some cases, the suffix **-ful** must be added to the root word before **-ly** is added in some cases. Not all words can have **-ful** added.

☑ Once a **-ful** suffix is added then **-ly** can be added.

Lens: Rely on Phonics

R

Rely on
Phonics

IMPROVING

Go Grapheme Grafters!

Spelling Practice

🕐 **20 MINUTES**

Please note all the words outlined for Year 3 cover focus areas in the National Curriculum.

Focus on these fifteen words on a cycle of two weeks, but go beyond seeing how they cope with the spelling, and target how to remember the tricky parts. This is not to be used as a spelling test. Teach spelling as a problem solving process; a mission to remember spelling for life. In the first instance, show pupils how to combine relying on phonics, then how to use visual and aural emphasis for the difficult bits. Personal problem spellings are identified and targeted through their 'Focus Five'. Encourage your pupils to be 'brave spellers' and to look closely at their mistakes so they can improve, with practice, and commit correct spellings to their long-term memory.

Learning
Look at the sound associations in the word knot. If a pupil can spell 'knot', then they know that \<kn\> can spell the sound /n/ in the following words: knock, knee, know, knife, knight.

Spell It Out!
Encourage your pupils to spell the words below correctly in their spelling journals. Can they notice that certain sounds appear in other words using the same spellings?

1.	knot	6.	knight	11.	marries
2.	having	7.	knot	12.	medal
3.	jacket	8.	last	13.	Mr
4.	jungle	9.	magic	14.	Mrs
5.	knead	10.	making	15.	munchies

For answers see www.thetrainingspace.co.uk/answers

Lens: Good Endings/ Suffixes

Good Endings/ Suffixes

GROUPINGS

QUICK!

10 MINUTES

When a **suffix** is added to a word, it changes the word class,
e.g. **slow (adjective)** to slowly **(adverb)**.

Learning
The suffix -ly is added to an adjective to form an adverb.

Words	
gentle	simple
humble	noble
feeble	nimble
subtle	supple
idle	stable

Question
Can you turn adjectives into adverbs by taking away the ending 'le' and adding the suffix -ly.

Lens: Group/Year Specific

Group/Year Specific

GROUPINGS

STICK!

10 MINUTES

Finding out which are more common choices sharpens our **'best bet'** approach.

Learning
The 'el' end for a spelling is much less common than 'le'.

Words	
'le'	**'el'**
castle	enamel
apple	camel
little	travel
eagle	towel

Question
Add your own. Which ending is more common? Find as many as you can.

Lens: Noticing Families and Roots

Flying Families

FLICK!

10 MINUTES

Can the baby owls pair up words that **sound the same** but **mean different things**?

A good pair is a **homophone** or **near homophone**.

he'll	main
not	mist
mail	peace
mane	plane
meat	heal
missed	rein
plain	meddle
piece	male
medal	knot
rain	meet

Lens: Go! Speed! Write!

Go! Speed! Write!

ACQUIRING

Exploding Potions

TICK!

10 MINUTES

In pairs you have the challenge to spell **10 words** correctly in a minute, or the potion bottle explodes!

Test each other across these **three categories**.

1 min Challenge	1 min Challenge	1 min Challenge
Numbers 61 - 80	Shapes	Toy shop themed words
Can you spell all 20?	How many shapes did you spell correctly?	How many words did you think of?

For answers see www.thetrainingspace.co.uk/answers

Lens: Interrogate and Check

IMPROVING

Spot the Spells

 **CLICK!** 10 MINUTES

Can you find the **11 spelling errors** in this piece of work and edit it to the correct **spellings**?

> **Dear Diary,**
>
> When I look on the calender, I can see there are two days untill Febuary. Some peeple think I am peculear that this is my favurite munth. It is dificult for me to discribe why I love it so much. Maybe it's becose Spring serprises are just around the corner.

1. ☐   4. ☐   7. ☐   10. ☐

2. ☐   5. ☐   8. ☐   11. ☐

3. ☐   6. ☐   9. ☐

Lens: **Syllables**

Syllables

GROUPINGS

Investigation 18

30 MINUTES

Hypothesis:

All **multisyllabic** words include words with associated meanings

Believe it or not?

Can you sort the example words into groups?

Multisyllabic words (smaller words with associated meanings)	Multisyllabic words (no smaller words with associate meanings)

Do you think the hypothesis is correct?

True 👍	False 👎	Sometimes 🖐

Pupil Page

Example Word List:

Teacher introduces some words to develop thinking. Use your professional judgement to introduce words during this investigation to push the learning on.

signature	potatoes
woman	celebration
children	basket
lonely	exercising
sixteen	umbrella
another	apricot
because	condiment
window	ambulance
balloon	different

Key Learning

☑ A **syllable** helps you break words into chunks.

☑ **Words within words** support you with extended and associated meanings between words.

Lens: Rely on Phonics

R

Rely on Phonics

IMPROVING

Go Grapheme Grafters!

Spelling Practice

20 MINUTES

Please note all the words outlined for Year 3 cover focus areas in the National Curriculum.

Focus on these fifteen words on a cycle of two weeks, but go beyond seeing how they cope with the spelling, and target how to remember the tricky parts. This is not to be used as a spelling test. Teach spelling as a problem solving process; a mission to remember spelling for life. In the first instance, show pupils how to combine relying on phonics, then how to use visual and aural emphasis for the difficult bits. Personal problem spellings are identified and targeted through their 'Focus Five'. Encourage your pupils to be 'brave spellers' and to look closely at their mistakes so they can improve, with practice, and commit correct spellings to their long-term memory.

Learning
Look at the sound associations in the word moustache. If a pupil can spell 'moustache', then they know that <ou> can spell the sound /ʌ/ in the following words: trouble, couple, country, young, courage.

Spell It Out!
Encourage your pupils to spell the words below correctly in their spelling journals. Can they notice that certain sounds appear in other words using the same spellings?

1.	moustache	6.	pause	11.	pours
2.	parties	7.	paws	12.	pretty
3.	pass	8.	penniless	13.	puppies
4.	past	9.	people	14.	quantity
5.	path	10.	plentiful	15.	royal

For answers see www.thetrainingspace.co.uk/answers

Lens: **Syllables**

QUICK!

10 MINUTES

Syllables are a unit of pronunciation having one vowel sound. There is **one syllable** in **light** There are **two syllables** in **wa/ter**. There are **three syllables** in **in/fer/no**.

Learning
Build multi multisyllabic words with 'ci' and 'ce' **'c' followed by 'i' or 'e' softens 'it'.**

Words	
ci	**ce**
cinema	ceiling
circumference	celebrate
city	celebrity
cinnamon	celery
circle	cell
circus	cellar
circuit	cement
circular	centipede

Question
How many words can you create? Listen to the sound, how many syllables?

Lens: Group/Year Specific

Group/Year Specific

GROUPINGS

STICK!

🕙 10 MINUTES

There are different **letter representations** for the sound **/uː/**.
Can you sort into three groups?

Learning
Same sound but different grapheme representations.

Words				
plume	June	Andrew	glue	screw
blew	tissue	blue	rue	crew
brute	clue	conclude	flute	rule
true	flew	brew	spruce	drew
sue	grew	knew	prune	flue
threw	fluke	rude	chew	issue

Question
Can you sort these words into the 3 groups?

'ue'	'ew'	'u-e'

Lens: Inspecting a Dictionary

IMPROVING

Dictionary Disaster

FLICK!

10 MINUTES

What a disaster! The words keep changing position.
Help the word wizard put them in **alphabetical order**.

Jumbled Order	Dictionary Order 1
1. disconnect	1.
2. disbelieve	2.
3. disappear	3.
4. disappoint	4.
5. discontinue	5.

Jumbled Order	Dictionary Order 2
1. straw	1.
2. strengthen	2.
3. strange	3.
4. street	4.
5. stream	5.

Lens: Order of Letters

Find your team

 TICK!

10 MINUTES

Can you sort the words into the correct 'team' when ending 'al'?

Learning
season   plur   tropic   refuse   logic   nation   internation   remove   post
adomin   lackadaisi   can   comic   bride   roy   ov   education   bury   topic
globe   centre   funer   carni   arrive   person   intention   bury   ped   magic
riv   fer   survive   emotion   me   soci   mamm   co

Word Wizard	Fairy Spell Mother
-al **as a suffix ending**	'al' **not as a suffix**
seasonal	plural

For answers see www.thetrainingspace.co.uk/answers

Lens: Navigating a Thesaurus

IMPROVING

Synonym Spectacular

 Red **CLICK!** **10 MINUTES**

Can you add in the missing letters for the words
in the same **synonym family**?

b _ _ _ k ➡ brisk

Fast	
1. a g _ _ e	5. s w _ _ _
2. n _ _ b l e	6. f l _ _ _ i n g
3. q _ _ _ k	7. f _ _ e t _ n g
4. r _ _ _ _	8. s n _ _ _ y
	9. h _ _ _ i e d

_ _ _ _ u a l ➡ gradual

Slow	
1. l e t h _ _ _ _ c	5. s l _ _ _ i s h
2. l e i _ _ _ e l y	6. c _ _ _ _ i n g
3. u n _ _ _ _ _ e d	7. p l _ d _ _ i n g
4. l _ _ y	8. l _ _ _ i n g
	9. s t _ _ _ a n t

Can you use a **thesaurus** to add more?

Medals of Mastery

Name:

Collect them all to become a Spelling Supremo

....

Instructions

Each child will be issued with a Medals of Mastery collection chart. As they complete the spelling investigations and activities, their progress can be marked on the chart.

Bronze Investigation Medal 1	Silver Go Grapheme Grafter Medal 2	Gold Fast Task Medal 3	Bronze Investigation Medal 1	Silver Go Grapheme Grafter Medal 2	Gold Fast Task Medal 3	Bronze Investigation Medal 1	Silver Go Grapheme Grafter Medal 2	Gold Fast Task Medal 3
Completed ☐	Completed ☐	Completed ☐	Completed ☐	Completed ☐	Completed ☐	Completed ☐	Completed ☐	Completed ☐
Week 1			**Week 2**			**Week 3**		
Completed ☐	Completed ☐	Completed ☐	Completed ☐	Completed ☐	Completed ☐	Completed ☐	Completed ☐	Completed ☐
Week 4			**Week 5**			**Week 6**		
Completed ☐	Completed ☐	Completed ☐	Completed ☐	Completed ☐	Completed ☐	Completed ☐	Completed ☐	Completed ☐
Week 7			**Week 8**			**Week 9**		
Completed ☐	Completed ☐	Completed ☐	Completed ☐	Completed ☐	Completed ☐	Completed ☐	Completed ☐	Completed ☐
Week 10			**Week 11**			**Week 12**		
Completed ☐	Completed ☐	Completed ☐	Completed ☐	Completed ☐	Completed ☐	Completed ☐	Completed ☐	Completed ☐
Week 13			**Week 14**			**Week 15**		
Completed ☐	Completed ☐	Completed ☐	Completed ☐	Completed ☐	Completed ☐	Completed ☐	Completed ☐	Completed ☐
Week 16			**Week 17**			**Week 18**		
Completed ☐	Completed ☐	Completed ☐	Completed ☐	Completed ☐	Completed ☐	Completed ☐	Completed ☐	Completed ☐
Week 19			**Week 20**			**Week 21**		
Completed ☐	Completed ☐	Completed ☐	Completed ☐	Completed ☐	Completed ☐	Completed ☐	Completed ☐	Completed ☐
Week 22			**Week 23**			**Week 24**		

Bronze Investigation Medal 1	Silver Go Grapheme Grafter Medal 2	Gold Fast Task Medal 3
ompleted ☐	Completed ☐	Completed ☐
Week 25		

Bronze Investigation Medal 1	Silver Go Grapheme Grafter Medal 2	Gold Fast Task Medal 3
Completed ☐	Completed ☐	Completed ☐
Week 26		

Bronze Investigation Medal 1	Silver Go Grapheme Grafter Medal 2	Gold Fast Task Medal 3
Completed ☐	Completed ☐	Completed ☐
Week 27		

Bronze Investigation Medal 1	Silver Go Grapheme Grafter Medal 2	Gold Fast Task Medal 3
Completed ☐	Completed ☐	Completed ☐
Week 28		

Bronze Investigation Medal 1	Silver Go Grapheme Grafter Medal 2	Gold Fast Task Medal 3
Completed ☐	Completed ☐	Completed ☐
Week 29		

Bronze Investigation Medal 1	Silver Go Grapheme Grafter Medal 2	Gold Fast Task Medal 3
Completed ☐	Completed ☐	Completed ☐
Week 30		

Bronze Investigation Medal 1	Silver Go Grapheme Grafter Medal 2	Gold Fast Task Medal 3
Completed ☐	Completed ☐	Completed ☐
Week 31		

Bronze Investigation Medal 1	Silver Go Grapheme Grafter Medal 2	Gold Fast Task Medal 3
Completed ☐	Completed ☐	Completed ☐
Week 32		

Bronze Investigation Medal 1	Silver Go Grapheme Grafter Medal 2	Gold Fast Task Medal 3
Completed ☐	Completed ☐	Completed ☐
Week 33		

Bronze Investigation Medal 1	Silver Go Grapheme Grafter Medal 2	Gold Fast Task Medal 3
Completed ☐	Completed ☐	Completed ☐
Week 34		

Bronze Investigation Medal 1	Silver Go Grapheme Grafter Medal 2	Gold Fast Task Medal 3
Completed ☐	Completed ☐	Completed ☐
Week 35		

Bronze Investigation Medal 1	Silver Go Grapheme Grafter Medal 2	Gold Fast Task Medal 3
Completed ☐	Completed ☐	Completed ☐
Week 36		

Spelling Supremo!

Congratulations

This certificate is presented to:

_____

for being a supreme speller.

Word Wizard   *Fairy Spellmother*

_____   _____   _____   _____
Date   **Word Wizard**   **Fairy Spellmother**   **Teacher Signature**

Teaching Sequence of an Investigation

ORGANISE	Set up how pupils will tackle the investigation
GROUPS	Can change over the year - individual, pairs and groups
RESOURCES	Relevant page from The Spelling Book, dictionaries/thesauruses/flashcards etc.

CONTEXT	Introduce the task/time boundaries
SET THE SCENE	Explain purpose of new learning Clarify vocabulary and use worked examples
PURPOSE	Consider what we already know Contemplate what we will find out

DEFINE	Set up the hypothesis to test
TERMINOLOGY	Identify key words in hypothesis Check understanding
TESTING THE HYPOTHESIS	Recap how to test a hypothesis Use technical language in context

MODEL	Showcase a set of words that prove or disprove
POSSIBLE STARTING POINTS	Suggest a couple of starting points Compare which seems most coherent
SUGGESTED PATHWAYS	Exemplify logical routes through the investigation

EXPLORE	Teacher's role fades in and out according to pupils' understanding
GUIDED EXPLORATION	Provide suggestions, kick-start thinking and play 'devil's advocate'
INDEPENDENT EXPLORATION	'Have a go' autonomously

CONCLUDE	Draw conclusions from testing the hypothesis
REFLECT	Consider what they now know
IMPACT	See how the new spelling findings impact the precision in independent writing

Teaching Sequence of a Fast Task

SET THE SCENE
· Define key vocabulary
· Lifelong word acquisition

CHALLENGE
· High expectations
· Time activity

SET THE SCENE
· Discover other words that exemplify point
· Explore exceptions and anomalies

SHARE
· Explain learning to each other
· Share findings with the class

Oh!

Oh!
Oh no!
There are rules,
You need to know... about oh,
Oh! I've hurt my toe,
Is an 'oe' sort of oh,

But if you moan,
Then it's an 'oa' sort of oh,

See the pain might grow,
And it's an 'ow' sort of oh,
If you're a sensitive soul,
Well it's an 'ou' sort of oh,
Toe injuries happen when alone,

This is an 'o-e' sort of oh,
Don't stub it again though,
That is an 'ough' sort of oh!

Jane Considine

Jane Considine Education

Do you want to be a better teacher of reading, writing and spelling?

LIFETIME ACCESS TO CONTENT

Let Jane Considine guide you through her practical, systematic and revolutionary systems in a range of online courses. Each step-by-step course will equip you with the knowledge and skills needed to implement the systems in your classroom.

All courses include lifetime access, so you can refresh your learning at any time. Once enrolled, you will have access to all course content, meaning you can set the pace of your learning.

Jane Considine online courses are available for:

The Write Stuff In the Early Years - Transforming the Teaching of Writing in the Early Years

The Write Stuff - Transforming the Teaching of Writing

Hooked on Books - Transforming the Teaching of Reading

The Spelling Book - Transforming the Teaching of Spelling

For more information and to enrol
visit www.janeconsidine.com

The Training Space